PROSTATE CANCER
A guide for patients

This book is endorsed by the
Prostate Cancer Research Foundation of Canada,
Canada's national research foundation solely
dedicated to prostate cancer.
The Foundation applaudes the efforts of
Dr. Laurence Klotz in creating
this comprehensive guide.

Coles Notes Medical Series

PROSTATE CANCER

A guide for patients

Dr. Laurence Klotz

Published by Prospero Books
2000 Toronto, Canada

© Copyright 2000 and Published by
COLES PUBLISHING. A division of Prospero Books.
Toronto – Canada

Cataloguing in Publication Data
Klotz, Laurence H., 1952–
Prostate cancer : a guide for patients

(Coles notes medical series) ISBN 0-7740-0609-9
I. Prostate — Cancer — Popular works. I.Title. II Series.

RC280.P7K56 2000   616.99'463   C00-930749-4

Publisher: Nigel Berrisford

Medical editor: Fred Saibil, MD, FRCP(C)

Editing: Paul Kropp Communications

Cover and book design: Karen Petherick
Layout and illustration: Christine Cullen

Printed and bound in Canada by Webcom Limited
Cover finish: Webcom's Exclusive DURACOAT

Contents

Appendices

Welcome to Coles Notes
Medical Series

The information explosion of the past 20 years has been especially striking in the field of medical science. Doctors and scientists have made tremendous progress in the diagnosis and treatment of all kinds of diseases, both old and new. Coupled with this progress, there has been a dramatic change in doctor-patient relationships. Gone, for the most part, is the old "just do what I tell you, and don't ask questions" approach to treatment. Patients are now asked to take responsibility for themselves and are encouraged to participate in the decision-making process when it comes to choices of therapy.

That's why we have developed a Coles Notes medical series. Like all Coles Notes, these books are informative and concise. Written in everyday, easy-to-understand language, they should provide you with the information that you need in order to establish an effective partnership with your treatment team.

All the author-doctors involved in this project are

eminent in their fields, and they all share a desire to educate the public about important medical issues. They believe that an informed patient (and family) is essential to modern medical care. An effective understanding means that you and your family have to be aware of the basic issues involved—from diagnosis of a condition, to the ways in which the condition may progress, to the currently available management strategies. The books in the Coles Notes medical series cover all of these issues. As well, these books guide you to other sources of information and support to groups across Canada. Each book has a detailed glossary at the back to explain those terms essential to your understanding.

It is our hope that these books will help you to be a better patient—or to be better equipped to support someone who is dealing with these medical issues. The treatment of a disease or condition no longer lies entirely in the hands of the physician. It requires your understanding, your consideration of treatment options, and your commitment to a treatment plan. We hope that Coles Notes will make this possible.

Fred Saibil, MD, FRCP(C)
Medical Editor, Coles Notes

Fred Saibil, MD, FRCP (C) is Head of the Division of Gastroenterology at Sunnybrook Health Science Centre as well as an Associate Professor of Medicine at the University of Toronto. He is the author of Crohn's Disease and Ulcerative Colitis *(Key Porter) and Medical Editor of the books in Coles Notes medical series.*

Introduction

Prostate cancer is now the most common internal cancer in humans. In the Western world, this disease directly affects one man in seven and indirectly affects almost everyone else when you consider the spouses, sons, daughters, friends and co-workers of affected patients.

It is also a disease that is characterized by patient choices at almost every step of the disease process. You must choose: Do I want to be screened for the disease? If I have prostate cancer, which treatments will I choose? You will have to make choices based on your values and priorities.

In order to make the right decision for yourself, you need to become informed about the facts of prostate cancer. This means learning about the way the disease behaves, the degree to which it is a threat and the degree to which it is not and the consequences of the various treatments, in terms of both the likelihood of cure and the impact on quality of life.

To communicate all this information to a patient is a challenge for the doctor. The challenge is even greater for the patient. When people are told they have cancer, their minds often go into panic mode. Other information that is given to them at that time frequently does not register.

This book is designed to help patients make informed decisions and for their family members to assist them in making these decisions. It is also geared towards people who have not been diagnosed with prostate cancer but are concerned about the disease. The evidence that prostate cancer can be prevented and steps that can be taken to do this are discussed in detail.

This book is dedicated to my patients, from whom I've learned so much and to patients of the future, to help them navigate the rocky shoals of this disease.

CHAPTER ONE

The Prostate

To understand the prostate, we should start a few months before the beginning—when you were still in your mother's womb. Early during fetal development, a small cluster of cells migrate together to form a gonad. This cluster develops into either the testis or the ovary. Which one depends on the chromosomal makeup of the cells. Females are XX, receiving one X chromosome from the egg and one X chromosome from the sperm. Boys receive an X from the egg and a Y from the sperm. In males the testicle begins to produce the male hormone testosterone beginning at about six weeks of fetal development. This hormone is powerful and has many effects. One of the most important functions of testosterone is to masculinize the internal reproductive organs of the body. Without testosterone, even in the presence of a Y chromosome, the female structures (for example, the uterus) are formed.

Testosterone is changed (by an enzyme called 5-alpha-reductase) to a more potent hormone, dihydro-testosterone (DHT). DHT causes another cluster of cells that are going to become the prostate, to develop into their normal form in the male fetus (see figure).

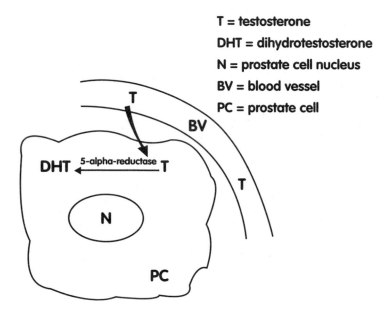

T = testosterone
DHT = dihydrotestosterone
N = prostate cell nucleus
BV = blood vessel
PC = prostate cell

Female fetuses have very little testosterone, so no prostate tissue forms. Interestingly, the prostate cell cluster remains in a very basic form and develops into the paraurethral glands of Skene, the female equivalent of the prostate.

A rare genetic change occurs in about one in 10,000 males that results in the absence of 5-alpha-reductase. Although the testicles develop normally, no DHT is produced. These genetic males grow up with normal testicles, but appear completely female otherwise.

Anatomy of the prostate

The prostate is present in most mammals. In dogs and humans, it surrounds the neck of the bladder and the urethra like a donut (see figure).

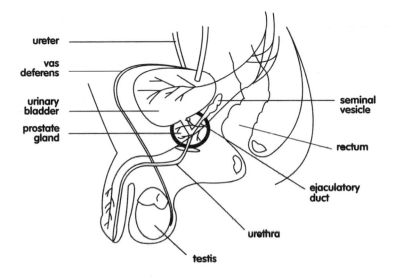

Most of the glandular (fluid-producing) part of the prostate lies behind the urethra (urinating tube). The part of the prostate in front of the urethra is small, consists mainly of fibrous tissue and does not produce fluid. The ejaculatory ducts enter in the middle of the prostate and drain into the utricle in the urethra. Ejaculatory fluid pours through these ducts into the urethra just before ejaculation. Fluid from the glands in the prostate drain into the ejaculatory ducts. Behind the bladder and draining into the ejaculatory ducts inside the prostate are the seminal vesicles. This pair of organs squeeze and push ejaculatory fluid into the urethra. Most of the ejaculatory fluid comes from the seminal vesicles. The relationship between the seminal vesicles, ejaculatory ducts and prostate are seen on the previous page.

The prostate contains three main kinds of cells. There are cells that produce secretions (liquids) that are added to the ejaculate; muscle cells that are involved in urinary control and ejaculation; and fibrous cells that help to provide the framework of the prostate.

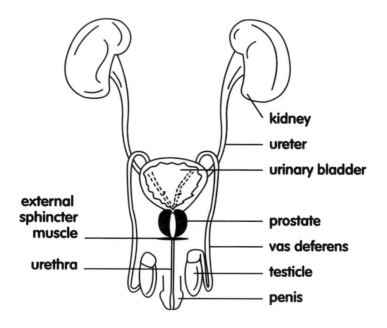

Functions of the Prostate
- aids fertility (supporting sperm)
- supplies nutrients for sperm
- inhibits bacterial growth
- liquefies coagulated spermatic fluid
- affects urinary control
- contains muscle that controls urine flow
- contracts to force sperm out the penis

The prostate sits at the junction of the urinary and genital tracts. Urine flows through the prostate from the bladder. The components of ejaculatory fluid are mixed in the prostate before ejaculation. This fluid is composed of three parts: the sperm from the testicles (about 10% of the volume), seminal vesicle fluid (about 60%) and prostatic secretions (about 30%). The seminal vesicles function primarily to produce nutrients for sperm. During ejaculation, the muscular sphincter surrounding the base of the bladder closes, preventing urine from passing down the urethra. The ejaculatory fluid (which is now composed of sperm and prostatic fluid) flows from the ejaculatory ducts into the urethra and is then pumped out the penis.

The prostate produces many chemicals that are added to the ejaculate. These include sugars, citric acid and a number of hormones, proteins, enzymes and trace elements, including zinc. The sugars and citric acid help provide nutrition for the sperm after ejaculation. The proteins and zinc form a complex that reduces bacterial growth and helps the sperm survive in the bacteria-rich environment of the vagina. One of the key enzymes secreted by the prostate is called prostate specific antigen (PSA). Ejaculatory fluid changes from a liquid to a semi-solid jelly soon after ejaculation. PSA is responsible for causing the ejaculate to change back to a liquid form and this is critical to the motility (ability to move) of the sperm. The relationship of PSA to prostate cancer will be discussed in detail later.

There are two kinds of muscle in our bodies—skeletal and smooth. Skeletal muscle is the kind that is attached to our bones; smooth muscle is present internally, in many organs and tissues. Smooth muscle in the prostate is involved in urinary control and ejaculation of sperm. There are three separate muscles involved in the control of urine flow: the internal sphincter, and the intrinsic and extrinsic components of the external sphincter. The prostate contains some muscle from the internal sphincter and much of the muscle of the intrinsic portion of the external sphincter. The internal muscles automatically keep urine in the bladder until you are ready to let it out, and they relax during urination. The external sphincter, which contains both kinds of muscle, acts as the "safety mechanism," and contracts when you have a desire to urinate and are trying to "hold it in."

Internal Structure of the Prostate

The prostate consists of three zones: the peripheral zone, the transition zone and the central zone. In young men, the peripheral zone makes up about 60% of the prostate. Beginning at about age 40, the transition zone, which is next to the urethra and makes up about 20%, begins to grow. This happens in all men as they age. This condition is called benign prostatic hyperplasia (BPH). Eventually, as BPH develops, the transition zone becomes the *biggest* zone of the prostate. The peripheral zone and capsule tend to be *squeezed* towards the back. It is important to note that (for reasons we don't understand) approximately 75% of prostate cancers arise in the peripheral zone. This zone is next to the rectum, and that's why many prostate cancers can be felt when we examine the rectum with a gloved finger. About 25% of prostate cancers arise in the transition zone or central zone, where they are harder to detect. These different zones can be seen clearly on transrectal ultrasound (see figure).

All three zones of the prostate consist of branching ducts lined by secretory cells that produce fluid, muscle cells and fibrous cells.

Diagram of prostate—three zones

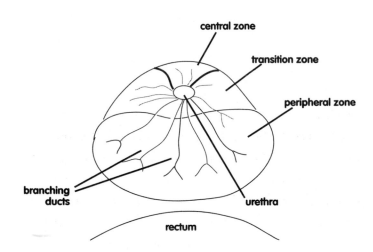

central zone

transition zone

peripheral zone

branching ducts

urethra

rectum

CHAPTER TWO

Non-cancerous diseases affecting the prostate

Benign Prostatic Hyperplasia (BPH)

Case history
Joe G. is a healthy 60-year-old man. For the last three years, he has noted that his stream of urine has started to slow down, and that he has to get up once or twice a night to urinate. He sometimes feels he can't empty his bladder completely. These symptoms don't bother him much, but he is concerned that they might be a sign of cancer.

In humans, the prostate begins to enlarge in mid-life. (Although most mammals have prostates, for some reason the only other species this enlargement occurs in is dogs). The process takes place in the transition zone. It is termed "benign" because it is non-cancerous (the cells that are produced look and act like normal cells). BPH does not lead to cancer. The term hyperplasia means an increased growth of cells. Although the process of

9

benign enlargement begins at different ages in different men, it eventually occurs in all men. The prostate volume in a 20-year-old is approximately 20 grams. Beginning about age 40, the volume gradually increases. By age 60 it averages about 30 grams, and by age 80, about 50 grams. In some men, however, it grows to massive proportions. The major consequence of this enlargement is that the urethra in the middle of the prostate is squeezed. This means that increasingly you will experience difficulty passing urine, a slowing of your urinary stream, a need to urinate more frequently, and an inability to empty the bladder completely. Some of these symptoms are also related to aging of the bladder itself. It is important to understand that problems like these are typical of benign prostatic enlargement and do not mean that you are at increased risk for prostate cancer. Virtually all men develop these symptoms eventually. In contrast, prostate cancer does not generally produce difficulty urinating until the disease has become very advanced locally.

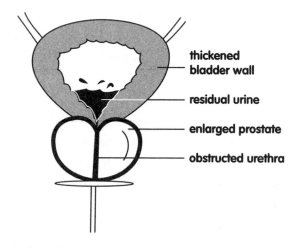

thickened
bladder wall

residual urine

enlarged prostate

obstructed urethra

BPH may also cause blood to appear in the urine (hematuria). This is usually painless. It occurs because as the prostate grows, blood vessels surrounding the prostate get very stretched and thinned and bleed easily. Such bleeding will often happen after straining, such as with forcing out a bowel movement. The amount of blood lost is usually small and not serious. However, if you ever notice blood in your urine, *tell your doctor*. This must be investigated to make sure there isn't a more serious cause, such as cancer of the kidney or bladder.

Benign prostatic enlargement is watched and not treated in mild cases. If the enlargement needs treatment, then drugs of several different types can be used. These include alpha blockers (Hytrin, Cardura and Flomax); 5-alpha-reductase inhibitors (Proscar); and herbal remedies (saw palmetto and others). An alternative to drugs is microwave heat energy applied to the prostate to shrink it. In more severe cases, the prostatic tissue causing the narrowing is surgically removed, either through the urethra (this is known as transurethral resection of the prostate, or TURP for short), or by surgery through the abdominal wall (known as open surgery).

The tissue that is removed is from the transition zone. This means that a patient can have a TURP that removes benign tissue while there is prostate cancer in the peripheral zone. However, it is important to remember that having BPH does not increase the risk of prostate cancer.

Prostatitis

Another common form of disease to affect the prostate is infection. The name for this is prostatitis. There are two types of prostatitis: acute and chronic. Acute prostatitis is an illness with high fever, severe burning on urination, an increase in urination frequency and a general feeling of being sick. Prostatitis is treated with intravenous antibiotics and usually responds well.

Chronic prostatitis is more common but less dramatic. The symptoms can include burning on urination, discomfort in the pelvic area, pain with ejaculation and more frequent urination. There is no fever and you don't feel sick. These symptoms can go on for months or even years and are often very resistant to treatment, which is with oral antibiotics.

It is important to know that these infections can cause the PSA to rise to very high levels. This may cause your doctor to think you have prostate cancer when you don't. If you have a high PSA due to prostatitis, the PSA should fall with antibiotic therapy. Because it isn't always easy to make a diagnosis of prostatitis, it may be necessary for your doctor to do a biopsy of the prostate to make sure it isn't cancer; the biopsy can show that the problem is prostatitis.

CHAPTER THREE

What is cancer?

Our bodies are composed of cells of many types: skin cells, muscle cells, bone cells and so on. Different cells working together form organs such as the heart, kidneys, prostate, etc. As fetal organs develop, these cells multiply rapidly. This growth is very carefully controlled by instructions carried in the genes inside each one of those cells. The instructions are affected by the local environment of each cell and also by signals hitting the surface of the cells.

After human beings have reached their full adult size, most organs don't get any larger. However, in some organs and tissues, old, worn-out cells are continually replaced by new cells. This happens in a very orderly and controlled way. Specific genes (you can think of a gene as a set of instructions) tell the cells when to die so that they can be replaced.

Cancer is an abnormality of the genes that results in loss of control of the orderly process of cell replacement described above.

Cancer cells have two characteristics:

- unregulated growth
- loss of differentiation

The loss of growth regulation can mean that either the cancer cells are growing faster, or too few of them are dying. Over the past few years, scientists have discovered that a common problem in cancer cells is a slower death rate of cells. Normal cells have a defined life span. They typically die by "programmed cell death"; the technical term for this is *apoptosis*. This is how it works: in response to a specific message, a suicide gene is turned on in the cell, commanding the cell to die. If this mechanism fails in a lot of cells within a short time, then the total number of cells in that area of the body is going to increase dramatically; the result is a tumor (lump).

Loss of differentiation means that the cell loses its normal structure and function. There are many different types of cancer, depending on which cell/cells are affected by the loss of control. Cancers often retain many of the characteristics of the tissue or organ in which they start. Adenocarcinomas arise from glands and are the most common; sarcomas arise from non-glandular tissue (like muscle, nerve or fat cells).

Normal cells are in communication with their neighbors. This communication helps them maintain their function and keeps them in place. Cancer cells stop communicating with their neighbors and become independent. The adhesive molecules that keep the cells in place are usually absent or lost, allowing cancer cells to move freely through tissue barriers and into the bloodstream (metastasis).

Cancer cells also have the ability to evade the body's immune system. Normally, white blood cells detect foreign or abnormal cells or proteins in the body and attack and destroy them (immune surveillance). Cancer cells often have the ability to hide from or suppress the immune system.

Most cancer cells retain some of the characteristics of their origin. For example, prostate cancer cells in most cases continue to secrete PSA, even if they have spread from the prostate into distant sites like bone. Another characteristic of cancer cells is that the genetic mistakes tend to accumulate more rapidly compared to normal cells. Typically, there will be an early mutation that will result in mild loss of regulation of the prostate cell. However, this mutation may also result in an increase in the rate of genetic mistakes. As the cell divides repeatedly, each generation of cells contains more genetic mistakes. The result is a highly cancerous cell, very different from its mildly abnormal great-great-grandparent. Cells that are very similar to the prostate cells that they came from tend to grow slowly. However, cells that have changed dramatically from their cell of origin have a tendency to grow quickly and to spread beyond the prostate.

This process of early genetic changes resulting in mild abnormalities leading to extensive genetic abnormalities and very abnormal and dangerous cells can take many years. An extended length of development is particularly true of prostate cancer. Recent studies of young men who died as a result of other illnesses have shown that the early changes of prostate cancer (dysplasia) are often present in the 20s and 30s. It can take 20 to 30 more years for these changes to reach the point where a prostate cancer is clinically apparent, and another eight to 10 years from that point to having life-threatening prostate cancer. In many men, therefore, prostate cancer is a slow-growing disease. However, the cancer can be very aggressive and rapidly fatal late in the course of the disease.

Because there is such a long latency period (the period when the cancer is progressing very slowly and accumulating genetic mutations), there is reason to think that the progression of prostate cancer from the latent to the active phase can be prevented.

What causes cancer to form?

Although there are now firm answers to this question, there are a number of clues that are leading us into further research. One clue is that the cancer does not form in men who are born with an abnormality in the levels of male hormones or in eunuchs (men castrated at a young age). Male hormones are required not only for the formation of the prostate, but for ongoing prostate growth. Over time, the exposure of the prostate cells to the male hormones (particularly dihydrotestosterone) leads to a greater chance of tumors forming. This is similar to the way in which long-term sun exposure results in recurrent skin tumors on the face. Manipulation of these hormones during the latency period (ages 40 to 70) may reduce the risk of prostate cancer. A number of genes have been identified that are involved in the development and progression of prostate cancer. One of these is called the p53 gene. P53 is often called the "sentinel of normality." It is a policing gene that keeps the cells under control and prevents tumors from forming. In a normal cell, if there is damage to the DNA (a gene mutation), then p53 is activitated. P53 causes the cells with mutations to die (undergo apoptosis). If the P53 gene is mutated or altered over time, the ability to weed out abnormal cells and to prevent tumor formation is lost.

Another group of genes are called *oncogenes*. "Oncogene" means "cancer-causing gene." These genes exist in normal cells, but are not activated. When they are turned on, they lead to unregulated cell growth and cancer.

Many environmental influences can determine whether these cancer-causing and cancer-preventing genes are altered. Male hormones are one influence. Diet is a second.

Diet and prostate cancer prevention

Many dietary compounds can increase the amounts of very reactive molecules called free oxygen radicals. These rampage inside a cell, binding to growth-regulatory molecules and to genes, resulting in mutations and alterations of cell growth. Free oxygen radicals are inactivated by other compounds called antioxidants. Antioxidants are scavengers for free oxygen radicals and inactivate them or escort them out of the cell where they do not cause any damage. In general, environmental or dietary compounds that increase the number of free oxygen radicals tend to increase the incidence of cancer; compounds that have an antioxidant effect, are often protective. An individual's exposure to more or less of these two types of compounds over many years undoubtedly influences the likelihood of developing cancer, including prostate cancer. These specific compounds will be discussed in the next chapter.

CHAPTER FOUR

Causes and risk factors

There are four factors that affect the likelihood that a man will develop prostate cancer.

Age

The risk of prostate cancer increases with age. Clinical prostate cancer is rarely seen under the age of 40 and remains uncommon until men reach their 60s and 70s. As the life expectancy of a population increases, the risk of dying of prostate cancer also goes up.

Race

The likelihood of being diagnosed with prostate cancer and of dying from the disease varies drastically among different races and countries. The disease is more common and more lethal in Blacks, intermediate in Caucasians and lowest in Asian men from China and Japan. To take the extreme example, the risk of an African-American dying of prostate cancer is about 100 times that of a Chinese man living in China.

21

There are several reasons for this. A number of genes that put people at greater risk of getting prostate cancer are at higher levels in Blacks than Caucasians, and higher levels in Caucasians than Asians. One of these genetic differences is in the androgen receptor, a molecule that binds to male hormones and is required for the hormone to activate the cell. The length of a certain part of this molecule, called the transactivation domain, determines how "turned on" the cell gets in response to a certain amount of male hormone. The longer this component of the molecule is, the less turned on the cell gets. The segment, called "CAG trinucleotide repeat," tends to be short in Blacks, intermediate in Caucasians and long in Asians. The shorter this segment is, the greater the risk of prostate cancer seems to be. There are also subtle differences in hormone levels between races, which may predispose some groups to the disease.

Family history

If someone in your family has had prostate cancer, then you have a higher risk of getting the disease than someone with no family history.

For example, if your father or brother has had the disease, then you have twice the usual chance of getting prostate cancer. If you have two close relatives with it, the risk goes up to eight times. If you have a close relative who was found to have prostate cancer before the age of 60, this increases the risk still more.

Some families have a gene for prostate cancer. This is thought to be on chromosome 1. In these families, virtually all men are diagnosed with prostate cancer. Luckily, these families are in the minority.

Diet

It is accepted that diet plays a role in the development of prostate cancer. The clearest demonstration of this is that the risk of prostate cancer increases in Asians who move from Japan to North America. Although the risk is still lower in Asians than in Caucasians living in North America and eating the same diet, it is about five times higher than in their relatives living in Japan. The most likely cause for this is an increase in fat intake.

Studies in laboratory animals have shown that the speed of growth of a prostate tumor implanted in a rat was faster in animals on a high-fat diet. Studies comparing men with and without prostate cancer have consistently shown a relationship between fat intake and the risk of prostate cancer. Most studies have shown that a high intake of animal or saturated fats increases the risk of prostate cancer by about two times. Some specific fats have been associated with this increased risk of prostate cancer, namely, alpha-linolenic acid and oleic acid.

Fat intake and prostate cancer

Why should an increase in fat intake cause prostate cancer? There are several possible mechanisms. Some fats are converted to eicosanoids, hormone-like fats made from linolenic acid in the diet. Fats can alter the body's levels of male hormones. During metabolism, they can form free oxygen radicals, which can interfere with the maintenance of normal cell membranes. Sensibly reducing your intake of animal fats likely decreases your risk of getting prostate cancer.

There are many other benefits to reducing fat intake. The risk of breast and colon cancer is also decreased by a low-fat diet. Heart disease, the most common cause of premature death in Canada, is partly related to dietary fat intake. It has been estimated that reducing fat intake by 30% could defer as many as 4000 deaths each year in Canada. The fats most likely to be at fault are those found in red meat. Since many diseases are related to a high-fat intake, it makes sense for all of us to reduce the intake of animal fat. Even if it turns out that this does not reduce the risk of prostate cancer, it is likely that your risk of other common and life-threatening diseases will be reduced. However, drastic reductions in fat intake should be avoided as other illnesses can result from insufficient fat in the diet.

Vitamin D

There is some evidence that a lack of vitamin D may increase the risk of prostate cancer. Vitamin D is converted into an active hormone, vitamin D3. This change happens in the skin with exposure to sunlight. Men who have reduced exposure to sunlight have an increased risk of prostate cancer. For example, Scandinavians, living in a northern climate, have one of the highest rates of prostate cancer in the world. Even if you are exposed to enough sunlight, your body may not make much vitamin D3. The skin of Black men contains melanin, which absorbs the ultraviolet light. Thus they have less conversion of vitamin D to the active hormone vitamin D3.

Prevention of prostate cancer

Humans are complex and sophisticated machines. We eat and drink nutrients and burn them in individual cells using complicated biochemical processes. Like any coal-burning or nuclear power plant, these energy processes produce byproducts, which may be toxic. Some of the byproducts are termed free oxygen radicals. These molecules have very high energy and a powerful tendency to join to other molecules in the cell. This causes injury to those cells. The injury may be in the cell wall, or in the nucleus, where the DNA is.

Our cells contain chemical defenses against free oxygen radicals. These chemicals join to the free oxygen radicals and change them into harmless compounds like water. The chemicals that make these molecular time bombs inactive are the enzymes glutathione-S-peroxidase, superoxide-dismutase and catalase. These are known as free radical scavengers. Free oxygen radicals can also be deactivated by some substances that mimic the action of these defensive molecules. These are called antioxidants and include selenium, vitamin E, vitamin A and vitamin C. Diets high in these antioxidants are associated with a lower cancer risk. We don't know yet if taking extra amounts of these antioxidants in the form of vitamin pills can reduce the risk of prostate cancer. Too much of some vitamins can be as bad as too little; *don't take large doses of vitamins or minerals without talking to your doctor.*

Selenium

Selenium is a trace element that is required for life. The amount of selenium in our diet varies widely according to the amount of selenium in the soil. In the body, selenium is incorporated into the antioxidant glutathione-S-peroxidase (S for selenium), which deactivates free oxygen radicals.

One recent study was carried out to see if selenium supplementation could reduce the risk of skin cancer; 1300 people with a low dietary intake of selenium were studied. Half of the patients took an extra 200 micrograms of selenium each day and half received placebo (an inactive pill). Although the selenium had no effect on skin cancer development, there was a marked reduction in the risk of developing other cancers, especially prostate cancer. The risk of getting prostate cancer was reduced by two-thirds, and the risk of death from any cancer reduced by one-half.

It is important to understand that the study did not set out to determine if prostate cancer was prevented by selenium. It is possible that this effect occurred for some other reason. At the time of writing we do not have established scientific proof that selenium prevents prostate cancer.

As well, there are risks in taking extra selenium. Selenium can produce side effects, including brittle hair and nail changes. It is even possible that selenium might increase cancer risk. More studies are needed to determine whether selenium intake is worth the risks and minor problems it leads to. However, if you decided to take selenium preventatively, the appropriate dose is between 50 and 200 micrograms per day.

Vitamin E

Vitamin E is an important dietary antioxidant. Vitamin E is present in vegetable oils, seeds, nuts and grains. In a similar fashion to the selenium story, the evidence for the possible preventive role of vitamin E in prostate cancer was discovered by chance. A study was carried out on male smokers in Finland to see if the frequency of lung cancer could be reduced. A total of 29,000 men were treated with either vitamin E and/or beta carotene, or placebo. There was no reduction in the rate of lung cancer, but the risk of prostate cancer was reduced by about 50%. Heart disease was also less common in the group on vitamin E, but there was a mild increase in the risk of stroke. What was just as interesting, however, was that the patients on beta carotene, another antioxidant, had a *higher risk* of prostate cancer. This study teaches us about the risk of taking vitamin supplements without adequate proof of their benefit. Beta carotene supplements increased the risk of both heart disease and cancer. While foods high in beta carotene may reduce the risk of cancer, extra beta carotene in pill form seems to be harmful. It does make sense to take a vitamin E supplement (about 400 units per day), as this appears to reduce the risk of not only prostate cancer, but also of heart disease. Several recent studies suggest that natural vitamin E pills are better than the synthetic pills.

Vitamin C

Vitamin C is also an antioxidant. While vitamin C has been shown to reduce cancer growth in some cell lines (cells being grown in a laboratory), this effect has only been seen at very high doses over prolonged periods of time. Studies in humans have not shown a reduced risk of prostate cancer with extra vitamin C.

Other foods that may prevent prostate cancer

Phytoestrogens

These substances are found in plants and mimic estrogens (female hormones). The most important of these are the isoflavones, and genistein is the most important isoflavone. Genistein is abundant in soybean products. There is much evidence that genistein can inhibit the growth of prostate cancer. This may be one reason why Japanese men, who have a high intake of soy, have a lower risk of prostate cancer.

Garlic

Garlic extracts have been demonstrated to decrease the growth of prostate cancer cell lines. However, the compounds used were derived from fermented garlic and are not present in fresh garlic. The impact of garlic remains uncertain.

Tomatoes

Isoflavanoids are also present at high levels in cooked tomatoes. There is some evidence that they are protective because of an estrogen-like effect. Raw tomatoes do not contain isoflavanoids in a form that is accessible to the body; cooking seems to release the compounds.

Vitamin D and prostate cancer prevention

Low levels of vitamin D seem to increase the risk of prostate cancer. Large doses of vitamin D increases levels of blood calcium. This can cause many other problems, including kidney stones and hardening of the arteries. Synthetic forms of vitamin D have been developed to try to produce an anti-cancer effect without any effect on calcium levels in the blood. This idea is still being studied.

Hormone therapy as a preventative

As we learned in Chapter 4, prostate cells require male hormones to grow and carry out their normal function. Without these hormones, the prostate cells lose all their functions, including the ability to divide and produce enzymes. Some prostate cells actually die in response to hormone withdrawal. This means that a reduction in hormone levels might reduce the risk of prostate cancer.

Testosterone is produced in the testicles. The hypothalamus (part of the brain) senses the amount of testosterone in the blood, and produces small amounts of a hormone called LHRH (luteinizing hormone-releasing hormone). This hormone in turn tells the pituitary gland (another part of the brain) to secrete LH (luteinizing hormone). LH tells the testicles to make testosterone. The hypothalamus acts like the boss in a manufacturing plant, telling the manager (the pituitary) to increase the production of testosterone by the workers (the testicles). Testosterone has many effects. It stimulates the growth of muscle and bone; causes the male pattern of hair distribution; increases acne; and alters behavior, particularly, interest in sex. Testosterone is the reason why men have a greater muscle and bone mass than women. In the prostate, the testosterone is converted by 5-alpha-reductase (see Chapter 1) to a much more powerful hormone, dihydrotestosterone (DHT). The DHT powers the prostate cell to grow, make molecules like PSA and divide. Without DHT, many prostate cells die.

These two hormones, testosterone and DHT, are important in the development of prostate cancer. Black men have a higher level of DHT than Caucasians, who in turn have a higher level than Asians. This correlates with the risk of prostate cancer. Because testosterone stimulates growth and multiplication of prostate cells, it is likely that large reductions in the level of testosterone and DHT would reduce the likelihood of developing prostate cancer.

The problem is that any reduction of these hormone levels has many side effects, including impotence, loss of interest in sex, and loss of muscle and bone mass. Recently drugs have been developed that only slightly reduce the level of testosterone but reduce DHT to a much greater extent. These drugs act by inhibiting the enzyme 5-alpha-reductase, reducing the conversion of testosterone to DHT. The drug currently available for this is called finasteride (Proscar). As finasteride reduces the amount of DHT in the prostate cell, it reduces the growth stimulus to the prostate. The hope is that this reduction will decrease the risk of prostate cancer, but we don't know yet if this will happen. A large study involving 16,000 men is currently underway, and we hope that the answer will be known by the year 2005.

Finasteride is currently being used for the treatment of benign prostatic enlargement. By reducing the levels of DHT in the prostate cells, the drug causes a decrease in cell size and about a 20% reduction in prostate volume. In patients who have large prostates blocking the flow of urine, this may result in an improvement of symptoms. However, the drug is less effective in most patients than a different class of drugs calls called alpha-blockers, which are used more often for this problem.

The result of a lower level of DHT in hair-producing cells in the skin is to stimulate growth in areas of male pattern baldness. This means that finasteride may reduce the likelihood of a man developing prostate cancer, can decrease the size of the prostate and can reverse the changes of male pattern baldness. Unfortunately, it does produce loss of interest in sex in some men. Until there is scientific proof that it does reduce the likelihood of dying of prostate cancer, it should not be taken preventively. However, it is reasonable to take it for treatment of BPH.

In summary, there are many reasons to think that clinical prostate cancer and death from prostate cancer are preventable. Since the early changes of prostate cancer begin in a man's 30s and are present in most men by the time they are 80, complete prevention may be too ambitious. However, if the rate of progression of these early changes can be slowed to the rate at which it occurs in Asian populations, both the rate of diagnosis and the death rate will drop dramatically. It is quite possible that by reducing animal fat intake, increasing protective micronutrients and antioxidants and increasing the intake of dietary supplements containing cancer-fighting molecules like genistein and isoflavanoids, this may be achieved. Attempts to prove this scientifically are needed and are underway.

CHAPTER FIVE

Detection of prostate cancer

PSA and early detection

PSA (prostate-specific antigen) is a substance made by the prostate gland and added into semen. Its function is to liquefy the jelly-like fluid after ejaculation. In normal prostate cells, PSA is secreted into the tubules, but a small amount leaks back into the spaces between the cells and ends up in the bloodstream. PSA is measured in the serum, the watery part of blood. With normal cells, most of the PSA stays in the tubule of the prostate gland and only a small amount gets into the serum. However, in prostate cancer, much more PSA gets into the serum. This occurs first of all because prostate cancer cells are often leakier than normal cells, and molecules like PSA spill out of them more readily. A second reason is that one of the earliest characteristics of cancer cells is loss of their alignment (polarity). In normal cells, the arrangement of the cells is very orderly, with the secreting part of the cell pointed towards the tubule. In prostate cancer, however, the cells are much more disorganized, and some of them can be pointed away from the tubule. This results in much more PSA getting into the serum.

This means that early prostate cancer can often be detected by a blood test that measures the PSA level. Most patients with a prostate cancer bigger than about 1 cm^3 (about the size of a sugar cube) have an abnormal level of PSA in the serum.

However, there are other conditions besides cancer that can cause a rise in the PSA. The most common of these is benign prostatic enlargement (see Chapter 2). This causes the PSA to go up, although only about one-tenth as fast per gram of tissue as prostate cancer. If you have a very large prostate, your PSA is likely to be elevated even if there is no cancer. Inflammation, usually due to infection, can also cause a rise in the PSA. This usually doesn't last long; the PSA returns to normal with treatment. Manipulation of the prostate, particularly from a medical procedure like a biopsy of the prostate, can cause a brief, sudden rise of PSA. The standard examination of the prostate through the rectum does not cause a rise in most patients, but can produce a moderate rise in a few. Recent ejaculation may also cause a short-term rise.

The half-life of PSA is about three days. This means that if a sudden event, like a biopsy or a digital-rectal exam, causes the PSA to go up, it takes five half-lives, or about two weeks for it to return to normal. This rise can be prolonged if a prostate biopsy produces some inflammation or infection.

In Caucasian populations, a PSA above 4 nanograms per mL is considered abnormal. But before you start worrying (if your PSA is over 4), read on about the effects of age and race.

If a general population of men over 50 is tested for PSA, 10% will have an abnormal level, and 3% will be found to have prostate cancer. This means that two out of three men with an abnormal PSA have a false positive test. In other words, even though their PSA is elevated, they don't have the disease.

This one-third likelihood of detecting prostate cancer from PSA actually compares quite favorably to most cancer screening tests. For example, the likelihood of having underlying breast cancer if a mammogram is abnormal is in the range of 20%.

Age

Since the prostate gradually grows as men get older, the PSA also gradually rises with age. For this reason many doctors adjust the cut-off between normal and abnormal PSA for the age of the patient. The current age-adjusted cut-offs used are the following: if you are in your 40s, the cut-off is 2.5; in your 50s, 3.5; in your 60s, 4.5; and in your 70s, 6.5. This means that the test will be more sensitive (more likely to diagnose the disease early) in young men. It also means that older men will be less likely to have a false positive finding (an

35

abnormal PSA in the absence of prostate cancer).

Race

PSA also varies (although to a smaller degree) with race. The following chart shows suggested PSA cut-offs adjusted for age and race.

Age and race-adjusted cut-off values for PSA			
Age	Caucasians	Blacks	Asians
40-49	2.5	2.0	2.0
50-59	3.5	4.0	3.0
60-69	4.5	4.5	4.0
70-80	6.5	5.5	5.0

Free versus total PSA

Several other approaches have been taken to try and improve the accuracy of the PSA test and to reduce the number of false positive results.

The most useful of these approaches is the free versus total PSA. This requires a little explanation. Because PSA is such a reactive molecule, most of what is in the serum is attached to another larger molecule called alpha-1 antichymotrypsin (ACT), whose job it is to deactivate the PSA. PSA that is bound to ACT does not interact with other molecules and therefore is prevented from wreaking havoc in the body. The amount of PSA that is bound to ACT is higher in men with prostate cancer than in men with benign prostatic enlargement.

The reason for this relates to the way that PSA gets

into the serum. In men with normal prostates, the PSA is secreted into the tubule and diffuses back into the space between the cells (the interstitial space). During that process, a little piece of the molecule is chopped off, rendering it less reactive. In prostate cancer, where there is loss of polarity, the PSA goes directly into the interstitial space and remains intact and more reactive. Thus the ACT binds more tightly to it. In other words, if you have a mild elevation of PSA, between 4 and 10, and the free PSA is less than 10, there is a 90% change that you have prostate cancer. If the percent free versus total PSA is greater than 24%, there is a 90% chance that you do *not* have prostate cancer. Ironically, men who are *free* of prostate cancer have more *free* PSA.

In practical terms, when a patient has a PSA between his age-adjusted cut-off of PSA and 10, many doctors will measure the percentage of free PSA. If it is high, no biopsy will be done; if it is low, a biopsy will be recommended. With this approach, the number of biopsies being done in this population falls by about one-third and 95% of the prostate cancers are still detected.

Another way to improve the accuracy of the PSA test is by using PSA density. PSA density is calculated by dividing the total serum PSA by the volume of the prostate as measured by transrectal ultrasound. As we have said before, if you have an enlarged benign prostate, the PSA is likely to be mildly elevated. Most men in this situation will have a PSA density less than

0.15. One serious problem with this approach is that a significant number of prostate cancers are missed. Many doctors only use PSA density for extreme cases, like avoiding a biopsy when patients have a huge prostate and only slight elevation of the PSA, resulting in a PSA density less than 0.10. Using the test in this way means that the proportion of patients biopsied unnecessarily would be reduced by about 10%, and only about 2% of cancers would be missed.

Sensitivity and specificity

These are statistical terms. Sensitivity refers to the likelihood that a patient who has the disease will have an abnormal test. Specificity refers to the likelihood that a positive test is caused by the disease being looked for and not by other factors. The sensitivity and specificity of any test are very subject to the cut-off that is used to decide what is abnormal. For example, if all patients with a PSA above 1.0 were biopsied, virtually 100% of prostate cancers would be detected, but about 70% of men tested would end up having a biopsy, many of them unnecessary. On the other hand, if a high cut-off is used, few men would get an unnecessary biopsy, but many prostate cancers would be missed. Another way of putting this is that the more specific a test, the less sensitive it is likely to be; the more sensitive, the less specific.

A different way to think about this is in terms of the positive predictive value, that is, the likelihood that someone who has an abnormal test will have prostate cancer. Overall, a patient with an abnormal PSA has about a one-in-three chance of having prostate cancer. If the PSA is between 4 and 10 and the prostate feels normal, the likelihood of prostate cancer drops to one in five. For a PSA above 10, the chance of prostate cancer is one in two. When the PSA is above 10 and a lump felt in the prostate, the likelihood goes up to 80%.

PSA Dynia

The first problem associated with the use of PSA to detect early prostate cancer is that about two out of three men with an abnormal test turn out not to have prostate cancer. These men suffer the anxiety that goes along with an abnormal screening test for cancer, as well as the discomfort and inconvenience of a biopsy of the prostate. Some men are able to shrug this off, but for others the abnormal test becomes a source of tremendous anxiety. This anxiety has been termed PSA Dynia (Dynia is the medical suffix for discomfort, in this case, the mental discomfort associated with an abnormal PSA). It is important to understand that most men with a mild elevation of PSA will never turn out to have prostate cancer, and that the decision to have a PSA done in the first place puts you at risk for this type of emotional upheaval even when a prostate cancer is not present. Tell your doctor that you don't want this test done without your permission.

PSA in the early detection of prostate cancer

PSA is the best test that we have for the early detection of prostate cancer. It results in the disease being treated at an earlier stage, when it is more likely to be cured. Although many men who have an abnormal PSA do not turn out to have prostate cancer, the test is more accurate than screening mammography for breast cancer and much better than screening tests for other cancers, like ovarian cancer. It also has the advantage of being a simple blood test, rather than requiring invasive procedures (such as colonoscopy for colon cancer). Unlike mammography, it does not require x-rays or a physician to perform it

Why is there such a controversy over prostate cancer screening?

The reason for this controversy has to do with the nature of prostate cancer (not the PSA test itself). Simply put, it has not been clearly proven that early detection of prostate cancer reduces the likelihood that an individual will die from the disease. There are clear benefits to PSA screening in terms of early detection. Screening with PSA means that prostate cancer is detected at an earlier stage, when it is more likely to be cured by appropriate treatment. However, whether this improved cure rate translates into a large enough reduction of the risk of dying of prostate cancer to offset the potential harm associated with aggressive diagnosis and treatment of early prostate cancer has not been proven scientifically. The reason for this is that prostate cancer is often very slow growing and is often diagnosed in older patients who have a limited life expectancy. Because of this, many patients die *with* prostate cancer rather than *of* prostate cancer. If you have a slow-growing prostate cancer and are destined to die of an unrelated cause, even without treatment, having this cancer diagnosed may result in aggressive treatment and its associated side effects without doing you any good. On the other hand, if your cancer is fast growing, early detection could save your life.

Large studies are currently ongoing that should prove this one way or the other. Until the answer is known, it is not appropriate to promote an aggressive screening program for prostate cancer. In the meantime, men should become informed about the risks and benefits of PSA screening (so they understand that it often involves a trade-off between quantity and quality of life) and make their own decisions.

Signs and symptoms of prostate cancer

Prostate cancer begins as a very few abnormal cells. These grow over the course of years until they finally become clinically detectable, usually when they are about the size of a sugar cube (1 cm^3). Early prostate cancer causes no symptoms whatsoever. Symptoms are things that you can feel and tell your doctor about.

Difficulty urinating is a symptom of prostate disease. Signs are things that your doctor can observe. A lump in the prostate is a sign.

Almost all men develop urinating symptoms as they age. These usually include getting up at night several times, slowing of the urinary stream, an inability to empty the bladder completely and a sense of urgency and difficulty holding the urinary stream back. These symptoms are not due to prostate cancer. They are caused by prostatic enlargement, which blocks the flow of urine, and by the aging bladder, which starts to squeeze sooner than it needs to (before the bladder is full). It is this combination of premature bladder activity and blockage of the flow from benign enlargement that produces these common symptoms. Most men who have these symptoms can be reassured that they are not symptoms of prostate cancer.

Only when prostate cancer becomes locally very advanced, and replaces most of the prostate, can it then cause obstruction to the flow of urine and produce obvious symptoms. Cancer should only be suspected in a patient who very suddenly develops urinating symptoms. In most people, these symptoms come on *gradually* over many years and only gradually become bothersome.

Prostate cancer does cause symptoms when it spreads. In 90% of cases in which cancer has spread beyond the prostate, it goes to the bone. Bone marrow contains many factors that stimulate prostate cancer growth. The bones of the spine (vertebrae) are the most typical location. This commonly produces back pain or pain going down one or both legs (sciatica). Prostate cancer also spreads to the lymph glands, and this may cause swelling of the legs. Lymph gland involvement in the abdomen may occur next to the ureters and produce kidney obstruction. Finally, the cancer may grow locally around the prostate. It can press on the rectum and make the patient feel the need to empty the rectum (have a bowel movement) more often, even when nothing is there. Rarely, the cancer can completely block the rectum, producing bowel obstruction.

Digital-rectal exam and early diagnosis

Case history

John C., 54, goes to his family doctor for a routine checkup. He feels well and has always been healthy. Last year, a normal PSA of 2.1 reassured him that he did not have prostate cancer. On this visit his doctor tells him that his prostate feels a little abnormal. He says that one side sticks out more and is harder than the other. His PSA is still normal at 2.3. John is referred to a urologist and is very concerned about this finding. What does it mean?

About one patient in four with significant prostate cancer does not have an increased PSA. In these people, a lump in the prostate gland is the only early evidence for the disease. Because most prostate cancers arise in the peripheral zone, in the back part of the prostate, they can be felt by a doctor's finger in the rectum. At a very early stage, prostate cancer may be felt as a change in consistency of the prostate. Normally, the prostate is soft or rubbery. Prostate cancer feels firm or hard. Loss of the groove down the midline of the prostate or an asymmetrical prostate, one side being more prominent than the other, may be early signs of prostate cancer. If you have these abnormalities you should have a prostatic biopsy, even your PSA is normal. If you have both an elevated PSA and an abnormality that can be felt

Digital-rectal exam

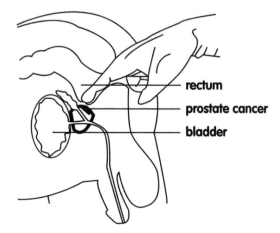

rectum

prostate cancer

bladder

in the prostate, this combination markedly increases the likelihood of having prostate cancer. The digital-rectal exam is also useful for finding abnormalities of the anus and rectum, including rectal cancer. It is considered a routine part of the physical examination, and should be performed by your family doctor annually over the age of 40.

In John's situation, the finding of an abnormal prostate is a clear indication to his doctor that he should proceed to a transrectal ultrasound and systematic biopsies of the prostate.

Transrectal ultrasound (TRUS)

The prostate can be seen very easily by placing an ultrasound probe into the rectum next to the prostate. This is a relatively painless procedure, no worse than having a digital-rectal exam. Transrectal ultrasound (TRUS) shows the different zones of the prostate and is useful for assessing the volume of the prostate. Cancers usually show up as a defect in which there are decreased ultrasound echoes. The figure shows a typical normal prostate and a prostate containing cancer.

Technique of
"TRUS-guided biopsy of prostate cancer"

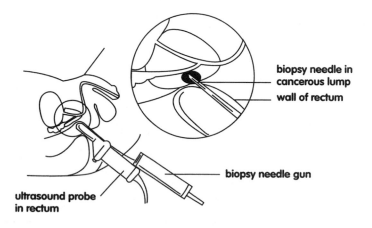

biopsy needle in
cancerous lump
wall of rectum

biopsy needle gun

ultrasound probe
in rectum

The main problem with the transrectal ultrasound as a screening test is that the specificity of the test is low. Areas of decreased echoes in the prostate ultrasound are much more common than the incidence of prostate cancer, and the likelihood that such a finding by itself indicates prostate cancer is only about 10%. Because of this, TRUS should *not* be used as a screening test. The main use of transrectal ultrasound is to guide the needle that is used to biopsy the prostate. Since the needle can be seen easily in the ultrasound images, the technique allows your doctor to systematically biopsy each part of the prostate. This makes it possible to thoroughly evaluate the gland microscopically.

Prostatic biopsies

When the PSA is elevated or a prostatic lump is present, the next step is a TRUS-guided prostatic biopsy. This is a fairly minor procedure that takes approximately 20 minutes. You do not need to be put to sleep for the biopsy. Patients take antibiotics starting the evening before the procedure and usually for a few days afterwards. An enema is used to clear stool out of the rectum one to two hours before the procedure.

The biopsies are taken using a biopsy gun, which very quickly removes a small core of tissue about 1 mm wide by 1 cm in length. This is performed at six to eight locations throughout the peripheral zone of the prostate. The operator uses the TRUS to ensure that all parts of the peripheral zone of the prostate are biopsied.

The main risk of a biopsy procedure is infection. This occurs in about one patient in 50; but such minor infections usually respond rapidly to antibiotic therapy. A few patients report persistent burning and more frequent urination for several weeks afterwards. Biopsies can also cause the PSA to remain elevated, sometimes for one to two months after the procedure, because of persistent inflammation in the biopsy sites. It is important to know this, because a sharp rise in PSA following a biopsy may be misinterpreted as an acceleration of prostate cancer progression.

CHAPTER SIX

If you have been diagnosed
with prostate cancer

Case history

Phil G. is a healthy 65-year-old. He is married with two grown children and has normal sexual function. He has no family history of prostate cancer. During his last routine annual check-up, his doctor told him that his prostate felt normal. Nonetheless, Phil was offered a PSA test by his doctor, and after reading an explanation of the pros and cons, he decided to have it done. His PSA came back at 8.5, and the free versus total PSA ratio was 0.10. He saw a urologist, and went on to have a TRUS-guided prostate biopsy that took six cores of tissue. This test showed a Gleason 6/10 adenocarcinoma involving 30% of one core and 10% of a second core.

For about two-thirds of patients with an elevated PSA, the biopsy ends up being normal. In this case, a second set of biopsies is sometimes obtained to ensure that the gland is truly free of cancer. Such patients need only do an annual follow-up to ensure that there are no further changes.

If your biopsy is positive, however, the real prostate cancer saga begins with a call from your urologist to come in to discuss the results. This next phase is absolutely critical, because dealing with prostate cancer involves making decisions that may well affect the rest of your life. If possible, a sympathetic family member should be present during this discussion to provide an independent perspective. Many decisions about treatment for prostate cancer involve trade-offs between quality of life and quantity of life. Your doctor's job is to help you become fully informed about the treatment options, and the risks and benefits of these options for your particular case. This is called shared patient decision making. The treating physician has a profound obligation to present you with the reasonable choices. Any doctor who says "This is the treatment you must have" is doing you a disservice.

What you should expect from your doctor

The physician (usually a urologist) should address the following eight issues in discussions with you:

1. grade of the tumor
2. stage of the tumor
3. significance of your PSA
4. impact of the various treatment choices on your quality of life, specifically with respect to sexual functioning and urinary control
5. the risk of your particular cancer causing major problems during your lifetime if it is not treated
6. the likelihood of cure with each of the treatment options
7. the likelihood of disease control with each of the treatment options if the cancer is not curable
8. risks of the major side effects from each of the treatment options

If physicians have a particular bias towards one type of treatment in general, they should be open about this. Many doctors in this field do try to be as unbiased and objective as possible in their assessment of the patient and in outlining the best treatment options. Your physician should tell you if he or she has a particular favorite treatment. If your doctor does not tell you, consider a second opinion.

Your doctor may be able to provide you with the risks of complications from his own personal practice. For a surgeon advocating a radical prostatectomy, ask about the likelihood of both significant incontinence and impotence from his own surgical practice. Ask how many prostatectomies he does per year. There is often a large variation between the results reported by major academic centers and those from surgeons who only do a few cases a year. The doctor who does radical prostatectomies infrequently may or may not do an excellent job, but he should be able to tell you (at least approximately) what his own results are. Similarly, the radiation oncologist should provide the risks of complications from her own hospital; this will be more meaningful than quotes from the literature, which typically come from major centers reporting the best case scenarios.

The significance of grade and stage

The grade of the cancer refers to the microscopic appearance of the cells. The stage refers to the extent of the cancer. If we compare a cancer to a house on fire, the grade would refer to the temperature of the fire, and the stage to the number of rooms that have been affected.

Although they are quite different, grade and stage tend to go hand in hand—low-stage cancers tend to be of lower grade, and high-stage cancers tend to be of higher grade. However, there are many exceptions to this generalization. Some of the toughest treatment decisions arise in patients with high-grade, low-stage cancers, or high-stage, low-grade cancers.

The grade of the cancer is assessed according to the Gleason system. This is a microscopic view of the architecture of the cancer. The Gleason Pattern is scored from 1 to 5, 1 being the most favorable-appearing type of cancer and 5 being least favorable. The rating out of 5 is based on the most common pattern in the cancer. The two most predominant patterns are added to give a Gleason score out of 10. A lot of evidence has shown that it is the presence of Gleason 4 or 5 pattern that indicates that the cancer has a tendency to spread and invade. Cancer with Gleason scores of 2 to 6 are usually considered favorable, with a high likelihood of cure. Gleason 7 (the sum of $3 + 4$ or $4 + 3$ patterns) is intermediate. Gleason scores of 8 to 10 are considered unfavorable with a low possibility of cure.

The stage of the cancer (or how extensive it is) is defined according to the TNM classification (see diagram on page 54). The T stage refers to the local extent of the cancer. N refers to the presence of spread to the lymph nodes, and M to distant metastases. For prostate cancer, distant metastases means it has spread to the bones in 90% of cases. Other sites of spread include the lungs and liver.

Staging of Prostate Cancer

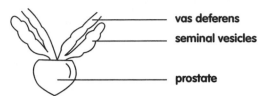

vas deferens

seminal vesicles

prostate

T1 (No palpable nodule)

T2A (palpable nodule involving less than half of a lobe)

T2B (palpable nodule involving more than half of a lobe)

T3 (extension into seminal vesicle)

T2C (palpable module involving both lobes)

cancer spreading locally

into lymph nodes

N1-3 (lymph node metastases)

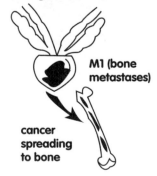

M1 (bone metastases)

cancer spreading to bone

The T stage is diagnosed mainly by digital-rectal exam. T1 means that the prostate that feels completely normal and that the cancer has been found because of surgery for a benign prostatic enlargement (T1a and b), or on the basis of an elevated PSA (T1c). The advent of widespread screening for prostate cancer with the PSA test has meant that stage T1c has become the most common stage at diagnosis, about 50% of new cases. Stage T2 means that there is a lump that feels, with a digital-rectal exam, like it is confined to the prostate. T3 refers to lumps of obvious cancers that feel as if they have extended beyond the prostate, either into or through the capsule, or into the adjoining structures, such as a seminal vesicle. T4 is very advanced local disease, which is fixed (the medical term for attached) to the pelvic side wall or rectum.

N0	No cancer in the lymph nodes
N1	Cancer present in the lymph nodes
M0	No distant metastases (cancer spread)
M1	Metastases present in bone or elsewhere

Staging workup

The presence of cancer beyond the prostate has a major impact on treatment. It is obvious that once the horse has left the barn, there is no point in closing the door. In other words, aggressive radical surgery on the prostate, which may make very good sense with localized disease offers little or no benefit to the patient in whom the disease has spread beyond the prostate. For patients at risk for spread (metastases), staging tests should be undertaken before a treatment decision is made. These tests may include a bone scan, CT scan and chest x-ray.

Bone scan

Since prostate cancer tends to spread to bones, a bone scan is essential. Patients at risk are those with at least one of the following: high stage, high grade or high PSA. Most patients with early localized prostate cancer are not at risk and do not require a bone scan. When the PSA is less than 10, the Gleason score is 6 or less and the prostate cancer feels confined to the gland or cannot be

 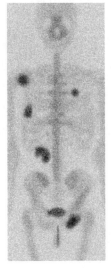

Normal bone scan   *Metastatic prostate cancer*

felt at all, the likelihood of finding metastases on a bone scan is almost 0 (about 1 in 300). Not doing the bone scan for these patients is one example where the PSA test has resulted in substantial cost savings. Before PSA, almost all patients with prostate cancer had to have a bone scan for staging.

CT scan

The CT scan is best for detecting enlarged lymph nodes. However, it has relatively poor sensitivity for picking up lymph node enlargement in the pelvic area, which is the first site of spread of prostate cancer. The same concept applies as for the bone scan. For patients with localized disease, a low PSA and an intermediate or low-grade prostate cancer, the CT scan is not done. It is only useful for patients with locally advanced disease and/or a high PSA and/or high grade in whom the risk of lymph node metastases is high.

MRI

MRI has not been shown to offer any advantage over CT in terms of assessing local extent of disease or lymph node metastases.

CXR

A chest X-ray will show areas of spread to the lungs (not common, but this occasionally occurs) and is an important part of the staging workup.

Prostascint

This is a new test that involves injecting an antibody directed against molecules on the surface of prostate cells. Antibodies are molecules made by immune cells; they have the ability to attach (bind) to specific molecules (antigens) on the cell surface. Prostate-directed antibodies bind, in theory, only to antigens on prostate cells. These antibodies are labelled with radioactive components that allow them to be detected by a scanner. When injected into the blood-stream, they attach to prostate cells, not only in the prostate, but anywhere else that the cells might have spread.

This test has turned out to be a more sensitive test for picking up lymph node metastases than CT scans. The problem is that it lacks both specificity and sensitivity. In other words, some patients who have a positive scan may not have prostate cancer cells in the lymph nodes; others with extensive prostate cancer in the lymph nodes have a normal scan. Because of this problem, it is not widely used. If it can be improved, it may become more popular.

RT-PCR for PSA mRNA

All cells in the body contain the DNA that codes for PSA. However, only prostate cells contain the RNA, which is the intermediary between the DNA coding for the protein and the protein itself. Reverse transcriptase polymerase chain reaction (RT-PCR) is a technique that allows the RNA coding for a specific molecule to be multiplied up to a billion times and, therefore, readily detected. Thus, RT-PCR can detect a single prostate cancer cell among tens of millions of non-prostate cells. RT-PCR can be performed on circulating blood cells to determine if there are prostate cells present. Since one of the characteristics of cancer cells is that they invade into the bloodstream where they are carried to other sites in the body, it stands to reason that finding cells with PSA RNA in the blood is an indication that the cancer has spread. Unfortunately, this test suffers from problems similar to those with Prostascint. Although a positive RT-PCR test for PSA is associated with a worse prognosis, there are frequent false positives and false negatives. It has not turned out to be a reliable test for staging.

Questions to ask your doctor

1. How advanced is my prostate cancer? What is its stage (in other words, how far has it spread)?
2. What is the grade of my cancer (how aggressive does it look under the microscope, and how quickly is it likely to spread)?
3. Do I need further tests? Why or why not?
4. Should I get a second opinion?
5. What are my treatment choices, including surveillance (just watching and checking every so often)?
6. What are the pros and cons of each treatment choice?
7. What are the chances that my cancer will be cured by treatment?

8. What kinds of complications can occur with each treatment? What is the probability of each of these complications? Are these probabilities from your own practice or from the reported literature?

9. How are these complications treated, particularly impotence and incontinence?

10. Will I have to pay for anything not covered by provincial medical plans or my insurance?

11. About how long will I be in hospital if I choose surgery? About how long will it take before I recover completely? What is the chance that I will recover completely?

12. How much time will be required for radiation therapy, if I need it?

13. What is the likely outcome if I choose no treatment (just surveillance)?

14. How often will I need to be examined while under surveillance?

15. Regarding surgery: How many radical prostatectomies do you perform a year? Is there a chance for nerve-sparing (see Chapter 8) in my case?

16. Regarding radiation: Do you use conformal radiation (see Chapter 10)? What dose of radiation will I receive?

CHAPTER SEVEN

Deciding on treatment

Shared patient decision making is a fundamental concept for patients who have been diagnosed with prostate cancer. Many patients and doctors are used to the traditional "paternalistic" medical model, where patients are informed of the diagnosis and of the treatment that they should have. In some situations, that is entirely reasonable. Where there is clear scientific evidence for one treatment that is superior to all others, and where there are no significant trade-offs, this works well. A patient with bacterial pneumonia who is advised to go on antibiotic therapy, or a patient with a fractured hip who is advised to have it pinned has received appropriate advice. This concept applies to acute diseases of sudden onset in which complete recovery is to be expected by treatment.

However, for chronic diseases, including prostate cancer, a much different set of expectations usually comes into play. The reason for this is that specific treatment approaches involve trade-offs and value judgments, often between the quality and quantity of life.

Quality of life is a complicated concept. Among aspects to consider are how you feel physically (very well, not so well, fair, poor) how you feel mentally (happy, frustrated, depressed, angry) your social life (going out whenever and wherever you want) and your work life (ability to perform your usual job).

Quantity of life is much simpler; it refers to how long you live.

The relationship between quality and quantity of life are different for every individual. The doctor who offers only a single treatment deprives patients of the right to balance these issues according to their own perspective. For example, it is a common situation in patients with cancer that they face the dilemma of choosing between aggressive and conservative management. Frequently, an aggressive approach involves treatment that has a considerable impact on quality of life. This may be acceptable because the goal in aggressive treatment is to increase quantity of life, often at the expense of quality of life. In some cases, the aggressive approach may be mutilating (for example, amputation), thus reducing the quality of life. The aggressive treatment may offer only a small chance of cure, but many patients (and their families) will go through anything to have a chance of cure, even if small. In contrast, a conservative approach often results in an improved quality of life for the duration of the patient's life, but no chance of cure, and a shorter survival time. The choice, ultimately, is yours.

How do patients choose?

It turns out that one of the most accurate predictors of whether patients choose to undergo aggressive therapy (even when there is only a small chance of cure) is the age of their children. A 65-year-old man who is married for the second time and has young children is much more likely to choose a treatment that offers him the chance of being around to see his children graduate from high school or university. The cost to him may be considerable in terms of quality of life, however. The treatment for prostate cancer may produce impotence or incontinence, but a person in this situation often considers the side effects as a small price to pay for longevity.

In contrast, a 65-year-old man whose children have left home and are independent, who has just retired and is on the verge of going around the world on a long-awaited vacation, tends to elect a more conservative approach that preserves quality of life. This is particularly true with a disease like prostate cancer, which is often chronic. The years of life saved are often 10 or more years in the future and may not be worth immediate sacrifices.

The choices will be a little different for everyone, depending on personal values and the trade-offs for each of the different treatment options in particular cases. Generalizations tend to be inaccurate. For example, sexual functioning is very important for some 65-year-old men and less important for others. These differences in values may be very hard for patients to describe accurately to the doctor, but they remain important.

Shared patient decision making

The job of the doctor in this situation is to help the patient become as informed as is possible about the risks and benefits of the various treatment options, and help him make a decision. Ultimately, the decision lies with you, the patient. Your family members may help you clarify your values in making the decision, but the final decision is yours once you get all the data in place.

Trade-offs

Prostate cancer is usually a slow-growing disease. For the average patient presenting with localized prostate cancer detected by a rise in PSA, it takes about eight to 10 years for the disease to become life-threatening without treatment. At that point, hormone therapy (discussed in Chapter 8) typically buys another few years. This means that the survival benefit associated with aggressive therapy usually doesn't kick in until about 10 years after the treatment.

If you are 60 years old and healthy and your life expectancy is more than 20 years, aggressive treatment is entirely worthwhile. You stand to benefit by about nine years of improved survival if your cancer is cured by treatment. *When adjusted for the decreased quality of*

Finally, it is probable that the population of patients treated in radiation series differ in subtle ways from patients treated with radical prostatectomy. It is certain that the watchful waiting studies are a highly selected, favorable group of patients. There is no way to effectively quantify this tendency (called selection bias). Nonetheless, it remains a possible explanation for differences seen in survival following treatment.

The major limitation of surgery has to do with the microscopic extent of cancer. The doctor's examining finger is not a microscope, and many patients whose cancer feels like it is confined to the prostate in fact have microscopic disease beyond the prostate. However, it is now possible to predict, based on the grade, stage and PSA, the likelihood that cancer that feels confined to the prostate really is confined, or has extended microscopically beyond the prostate, extended to lymph nodes or involves the seminal vesicles. This information is tabulated in the Partin tables (see the next page for a simplified chart). Using these tables, a patient with a given PSA, grade and stage can be told the likelihood of having organ-confined disease, cancer at the outside of the surgical specimen (positive surgical margins), and seminal vesicle and lymph node involvement (this is called pathological staging). This information is very helpful to your decision making.

Partin Tables

These are simplified versions of the more complex Partin tables available to your doctor. These tables predict the percentage chance that a cancer has established beyond the prostate based on PSA results and Gleason Score.

PSA 0-4.0 Percent likelihood of eEstablished capsular penetration

Gleason Score	T1c	T2a	T2b	T2c
2-4	10	18	25	21
5	18	30	40	34
6	21	34	43	37
7	31	45	51	45
8-10	34	47	48	42

PSA 0-4.0 Percent likelihood of lymph node involvement

Gleason Score	T1c	T2a	T2b	T2c
2-4	0	0	0	0
5	0	0	1	1
6	0	1	2	2
7	1	2	5	5
8-10	4	5	10	10

PSA 4-10 Percent likelihood of established capsular penetration

Gleason Score	T1c	T2a	T2b	T2c
2-4	15	26	35	29
5	27	41	50	43
6	30	44	52	46
7	40	52	54	48
8-10	40	49	46	40

PSA 4-10 Percent likelihood of lymph node involvement

Gleason Score	T1c	T2a	T2b	T2c
2-4	0	0	1	1
5	0	1	2	2
6	1	2	4	4
7	3	4	9	9
8-10	8	9	16	17

PSA 10-20 Likelihood of established capsular penetration

Gleason Score	T1c	T2a	T2b	T2c
2-4	22	35	43	37
5	35	50	57	51
6	38	52	57	50
45	45	55	51	45
8-10	40	46	38	33

PSA 10-20 Likelihood of lymph node involvement

Gleason Score	T1c	T2a	T2b	T2c
2-4	0	1	1	1
5	1	2	4	4
6	3	4	10	10
7	8	9	17	18
8-10	16	17	29	29

PSA > than 20 Likelihood of established capsular penetration

Gleason Score	T1c	T2a	T2b	T2c
2-4	34	48	52	—
5	48	60	61	55
6	49	60	57	51
7	46	51	43	37
8-10	34	47	28	23

PSA > than 20 Likelihood of lymph node involvement

Gleason Score	T1c	T2a	T2b	T2c
2-4	1	1	3	—
5	3	3	7	7
6	7	8	16	17
7	14	14	25	25
8-10	24	24	36	35

However, the pitfall of this approach is that the table only provides information on pathologic staging, or extent of the disease. What patients really want to know is how likely they are to be cured by surgery. There is not a direct correlation between the pathologic extent of the cancer and the likelihood of cure. With organ-confined disease, the likelihood of long-term cure is at least 90%. With extension beyond the capsule but a negative surgical margin, that drops to 70%. With a positive surgical margin, 50% of patients are still cured and with seminal vesicle involvement 30% are cured. In other words, the likelihood of cure, if the disease has extended beyond the prostate, must be taken into account as well as the likelihood that it has extended at all. It is your doctor's job to make sure that you have all the information you need on this issue.

CHAPTER EIGHT

Surgery for prostate cancer

There are three common operations available for dealing with prostate cancer, and other surgical procedures that might be of some use. This chapter will explain each of them.

Radical retropubic prostatectomy

Preoperative preparation: Your surgery may be booked in advance by the surgeon, or you may be placed on a waiting list and called when a bed and operating time become available. You may be seen in a pre-admission clinic several weeks in advance of your operation. At that time, you will have blood work, an electrocardiogram and a chest x-ray. You'll also see an anesthetist, particularly if you have some other health problems, and provide identification and basic personal information. Be prepared—this process may be quite time consuming. Many surgeons have patients donate one or two units of their own blood, which is stored and can be administered during surgery. This reduces the likelihood of a patient requiring transfusion from a third party to virtually zero.

The day prior to surgery: Your bowel is cleaned out using a milkshake of magnesium citrate or an electrolyte solution. Patients must take nothing by mouth eight hours prior to the surgery (most anesthetists will allow a sip of water with pills to be taken on the morning of surgery if necessary).

The day of surgery: You will be anesthetized with either a general (you will be asleep) or spinal anesthetic (frozen from the waist down). The operation is performed with patients on their back lying flat or with the legs up in stirrups. An incision is made in the midline from just below the navel down to the pubic bone. A retractor is put in place to hold the edges of the wound apart. The vas deferens (tubes leading the sperm from the testes) are tied off.

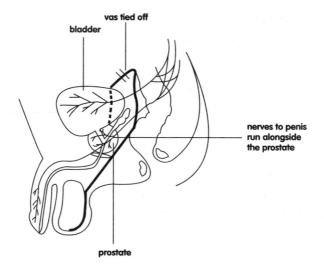

The lymph nodes draining the prostate are removed in selected cases. The Partin tables are used here in making decisions on the operation. For combinations of grade, stage and PSA where the likelihood of spread to the lymph nodes is 3% or less, this step is skipped by most surgeons.

Radical retropubic prostatectomy

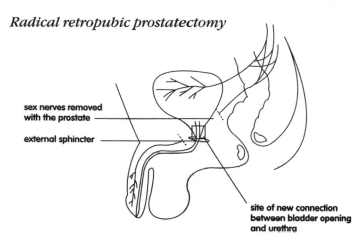

sex nerves removed with the prostate

external sphincter

site of new connection between bladder opening and urethra

After exposing the prostate low down in the pelvis, the veins on top of the prostate are sutured. The next critical step is to clamp or suture the dorsal vein complex, a bundle of veins draining blood from the penis and deep pelvis. These veins lie right on top of the urethra and cross next to the sphincter responsible for urinary control. It is critical that this complex be tied off correctly, in a way that will minimize bleeding after the veins are divided and not interfere with the function of the sphincter mechanism. This is where surgical experience is critical. After dividing the dorsal vein complex, the urethra (the tube carrying the urine) is cut immediately below the prostate. This is the second crucial step. If the urethra is cut too close to the prostate, prostate cancer may be left behind. If it is cut too far away, problems with urinary control may be the result. The tissue holding the prostate in place on either side is then clipped or tied off and cut. This is where the nerve-sparing technique comes into play.

Nerve-sparing prostatectomy

The cavernous nerves, which are responsible for erections, run immediately next to the prostate, where the prostate meets the rectum. They run parallel to the back part of the prostate and immediately next to the urethra. These nerves are smaller than a human hair and not readily visible in most patients. However, they run in a bundle of structures that includes blood vessels and this bundle is usually readily visible. The nerve-sparing operation involves shaving very close to the prostate in order to preserve the neurovascular (nerve-blood vessel) bundle.

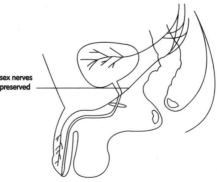

sex nerves
preserved

*Nerve-sparing
prostatectony*

The obvious risk of the nerve-sparing technique is that by shaving so close to the prostate, cancer cells may be left behind. In properly selected patients (with low stage, grade and PSA), this risk has been demonstrated to be quite small, about 5%. However, candidates with more advanced disease should not have a nerve-sparing approach. This issue of nerve-sparing versus no nerve-sparing should be addressed prior to patients undertaking the surgery.

The results of nerve-sparing

The rationale behind nerve-sparing is simple: it preserves sexual functioning. However, the results in terms of potency preservation vary widely among surgeons. The best results, from Johns Hopkins (in Baltimore), indicate that for about 90% of patients under the age of 60 undergoing a nerve-sparing prostatectomy, their potency will be preserved. However, most surgeons are unable to replicate these results. For most surgeons, the nerve-sparing prostatectomy in men who have normal erections prior to surgery results in about half the patients retaining potency after the operation. It is important to understand that the quality of these erections is usually inferior to those prior to surgery, although still adequate for normal intercourse.

A new technique may improve nerve-sparing results. The Cavermap consists of a nerve-stimulating device and a sensitive strain gauge placed around the base of the penis. During surgery, the surgeon stimulates in the area of the neurovascular bundle prior to dividing the tissue. If the nerve is present in this tissue, 15 to 20 seconds of stimulation will produce a slight enlargement of the penis. This technique can be used to map the course of the nerve. Where stimulation of an area about to be divided results in an increase in penile girth (tumescence), the surgeon moves a little closer to the prostate and tries stimulating again. This technique has been shown in a randomized trial to result in improved potency preservation rates. Further experience will be required before this device becomes part of standard therapy.

Following the division of the lateral pedicles, the seminal vesicles are dissected out and the prostate is cut away from the bladder and removed. The opening in the bladder is then tapered, if necessary, and sutured down to the urethra over a catheter (a rubber tube placed into the urethra through the opening in the penis). The incision is closed. A drain is left in place to take away any urine that might leak out of the joining of the bladder and urethra.

The catheter is usually left in place approximately two to three weeks. The drain is typically removed on the second to third day after surgery and the patient usually goes home on the third or fourth day. The clips or sutures in the skin are removed seven to nine days following surgery.

Perineal prostatectomy

This operation involves essentially the same manoeuvres as the retropubic prostatectomy. In this procedure, however, the incision is made between the legs under the scrotum. From this entry point, the lower end of prostate is much more accessible but the bladder neck and base of the prostate are less accessible.

The advantages of the perineal approach are less post-operative pain and a somewhat more rapid discharge from hospital (two or three days). There is, for most patients, less blood loss. The disadvantage is that your anatomy is not as clearly seen by your doctor. The lateral pedicles and seminal vesicles and bladder neck are seen more clearly using the retropubic approach and the dissection is more precise and anatomical.

Most surgeons tend to favor one approach or the other. The results in skilled hands seem to be equivalent. The retropubic approach is much more popular in the United States and Canada.

Because the abdominal incision delays the return to strenuous work, the perineal approach makes sense in individuals who are very anxious to return to full manual work as soon as possible after surgery. It also makes sense for patients who have had multiple abdominal operations with extensive scar tissue formation.

Other operations (TURP)

TURP (transurethral prostatectomy) involves removal of the transition zone of the prostate by an instrument placed in the urethra. This is not a cancer operation, but instead is used to improve urinating for patients who have some obstruction. It is occasionally used as a palliative operation for patients who have locally advanced prostate cancer prior to or following radiation therapy or hormone therapy. It is not and should not be considered as a definitive cancer operation.

What you can expect after surgery

Early

The technique of patient-controlled analgesia (PCA) has transformed the experience of many patients after surgery. A pump, controlled by the patient, delivers pain-killing medication intravenously whenever a button is pressed. This means that, for the first few days after surgery, pain can be kept to a bare minimum. PCA has become the standard approach to pain management after surgery in most major institutions. Secondly, non-steroidal anti-inflammatory drugs (NSAIDs) are used routinely instead of more powerful opioids like morphine. This has resulted in a much more rapid return of bowel function and earlier discharge from hospital.

After the operation, a drain is left in place in case there is a leak of urine from the anastomosis (the connection of the bladder and urethra). If this occurs, it may delay discharge for a few days. Rarely, the patient will be sent home with the drain in place. These leaks are not serious and almost always get better on their own.

The patient is usually sent home with a catheter draining the bladder. This is attached to a bag wrapped around the leg during the day and a larger bag by the side of the bed at night. It is easy to manage and does not require special nursing care.

The catheter is removed two to three weeks after surgery. Most patients will have some degree of incontinence immediately after catheter removal. This resolves over time, requiring one to three months. Patients should be prepared for this both physically (wear casual dark pants when seeing the doctor for catheter removal and have some pads on hand) and psychologically. It is important to remember that the incontinence experienced immediately after catheter removal improves and usually resolves over time.

Long term

In skilled hands, only about 10% of patients will require pads or other incontinence devices. In most of these patients, the degree of incontinence is fairly mild. However, in 2% of patients, statistically, the incontinence is severe. These patients become candidates for an artificial sphincter.

Men opting for a surgical treatment should be prepared, unfortunately, for a slightly diminished level of continence than normal. The degree of incontinence typically approximates that of normal middle-aged women (many middle-aged women with a full bladder will lose a drop of urine in response to a hard cough). This degree of incontinence is common following prostatectomy. However, it is not a social problem and does not require significant adjustment.

As surgeons have gained more experience with radical prostatectomy and refinements have been embraced, the outcome in terms of continence has improved substantially. Although most patients have complete or near complete levels of continence after surgery, a small proportion have long-term impairment of continence. This needs to be appreciated as the major risk factor following surgery. Risk factors for incontinence are increased age, obesity and chronic lung disease (particularly if a chronic cough is a component of it). Such patients should seriously consider non-surgical alternatives as primary treatment for their cancer.

Impotence

This is the most common long-term side effect of surgery for prostate cancer. Even with a nerve-sparing procedure, most patients have impotence for several months after surgery. For patients whose nerves are spared, erections may recover over a period of six to 12 months. Occasionally, potency takes up to two years to recover.

In the absence of a nerve-sparing operation and even

with this technique, potency will often be completely absent.

Recent data suggests that one reason for long-term impotence (particularly after a nerve-sparing approach) is that, for several months after surgery, the absence of spontaneous erections leads to reduced blood flow to the penis. This results in scarring or fibrosis of the tissue responsible for erection. Some doctors refer to this as the "use it or lose it" hypothesis.

There is some evidence that restoring increased blood flow during this period by the use of injections into the penis will improve the likelihood of long-term recovery of spontaneous erections. Thus, patients who are concerned about potency after surgery should use either intercorporeal injection, or the Muse intraurethral pellet. The concept is to restore erections with drugs while waiting for them to recover spontaneously. This should begin about two to four months after surgery. Studies suggest that intracorporeal injection will improve the recovery of spontaneous erections. While Viagra may also restore blood flow and thereby improve eventual recovery of erections, there is not proof of this yet.

Viagra

Viagra works by inhibiting phosphodiesterase, which is a molecule that normally degrades nitric oxide (which is responsible for increased penile blood flow). For Viagra to work, the signal to increase nitric oxide must be present in the first place. Viagra is usually only effective in patients who have had a nerve-sparing prostatectomy. Fifty to 80% of patients who are impotent following a nerve-sparing prostatectomy will respond to Viagra with some recovery of erections. The success rate is lower in older patients. These results remain to be proven by larger studies, but many patients decide that it is certainly worth trying the drug.

Bladder neck contracture

Scar tissue develops at the connection between the bladder neck and the urethra in about 10% of patients. This results in a narrowing of the opening of the bladder neck, and that leads to increased difficulty in urinating and slowing of the urine stream. Such problems can be easily dealt with by putting an instrument (cystoscope) up the urethra and cutting the scar tissue (contracture) under direct vision. This procedure takes between five and 10 minutes and can be performed under local anaesthesia. In most cases, a single procedure is sufficient to definitively deal with the contracture. Occasionally, patients will require repeated incisions or a more extensive procedure under anesthesia. This is rarely a recurrent problem.

CHAPTER NINE

The pathology report

When you return to your urologist for the catheter removal, your pathology report should be reviewed carefully. This information is used to predict the likelihood of recurrence of prostate cancer, and the need for further treatment. These are the items in the report:

Gleason score

The Gleason score of the entire cancer (rather than of the sampling taken on biopsy) is documented. The Gleason score on the entire specimen may differ from that on the biopsy. This is particularly true if hormone therapy has been used to shrink the prostate prior to surgery. Hormone therapy before surgery tends to artificially increase the Gleason score of the cancer. This is an artifact of the hormone treatment and does not mean that the cancer has become worse.

Pathologic stage (actual extent of the cancer)

The important aspects of the pathologic stage are the presence of positive surgical margins, seminal vesicle involvement and positive lymph nodes. Capsular penetration (whether the cancer has extended through the capsule) is not very significant in terms of the likelihood of recurrence, if the cancer is surrounded by normal tissue. However, if the specimen that has been removed has cancer at the outside of the specimen (positive surgical margin), there is a relatively high chance that cancer has been left behind. The risk of recurrence with a negative surgical margin, even with capsular penetration, is 30%; with a positive surgical margin, 50 to 60%.

The extension of the cancer into the seminal vesicles indicates aggressive cancer biologically and is associated with a 70% recurrence rate.

The presence of cancer in the regional lymph nodes almost always indicates that the cancer is incurable. Without further treatment, 95% of these patients will suffer recurrence. In general, patients with lymph node metastases following prostatectomy are also treated with hormone therapy. This results in long-term disease suppression and may cure some patients.

Patients with extensive positive margins or seminal vesicle involvement may benefit from external beam radiation given after they have recovered from the surgery.

Follow-up after surgery

In 90% of patients, the PSA falls to undetectable levels (less than 0.1 ng/mL). Following surgery, the PSA is an extremely sensitive test for recurrence. In addition, the time between the operation and the subsequent rise in PSA provides information about where the disease has recurred, if it does.

In some patients, the PSA fails to fall to undetectable levels after surgery, or begins to rise within one year. Ninety percent of such patients turn out to have microscopic spread of prostate cancer to either the bones or lymph nodes. Fortunately this is not common. More frequently, the PSA begins to rise one to seven years following the prostatectomy (the average is three years). Under those circumstances, the majority turn out to have only a local recurrence. This means that the cancer has grown back in the bed of the prostate.

These patients may still be cured by external beam radiation to the bed of the prostate. If the radiation is given as soon as the PSA begins to rise (before it reaches 2.0 ng/mL), there is a 50% chance that the PSA will fall to undetectable levels again and the patient will remain free of recurrence.

Most doctors carefully observe patients after surgery to see what happens to the PSA, even if there are positive margins or seminal vesicle involvement. Some patients with these adverse findings are still cured by surgery alone. If the PSA fails to become undetectable or begins to rise within a year, the patients are treated with long-term hormonal therapy. Conversely, if the PSA remains undetectable for more than a year and then rises, the patients are treated with radiation to the bed of the prostate. In very high-risk or very young patients with adverse pathology, the radiation may be given even with an undetectable PSA, usually beginning about three months after surgery.

Once the PSA has been undetectable for seven years, the chance of recurrence of prostate cancer is virtually zero.

A rise in PSA after surgery is still compatible with long-term survival. In a recent study of 2000 patients from Johns Hopkins, the average time from PSA recurrence after surgery to metastatic disease was eight years, and from metastatic disease to death five years. Since the average time to PSA recurrence was three years, the patients failing curative surgery still lived for an average of 16 years. This important observation emphasizes the long-term survival of patients living with prostate cancer.

CHAPTER TEN

Radiation therapy

The use of ionizing radiation to destroy cancerous tissue has a proven role in the treatment of many cancers. Radiation works by causing breaks in the genes (DNA) of cells. This leads to a loss in the ability of the cells to divide and eventually results in their death. Since cancer cells have a faster growth rate than normal cells, they are more sensitive to radiation.

Radiation can be produced naturally or artificially. Artificially produced radiation includes the use of isotopes such as cobalt-60, iodine-125 and strontium-89. These isotopes are produced by bombarding inactive elements with neutrons. Some hospitals make use of external beam radiation produced by linear accelerators.

Radiation treatment can be given in one of two ways: by direct implantation of radioactive compounds into the prostate (brachytherapy) or by an external beam of radiation directed at the prostate. Some hospitals use a combination of external beam irradiation and radio-active "seed" implantation. (At the time of writing, combination therapy is not being used in Canada.)

Brachytherapy

This treatment is administered by implanting radioactive material into the prostate. Brachytherapy can be done using 'seeds'—thin metal containers the size of a grain of rice which are filled with the radioactive compound,—permanently placed through a needle into the prostate. It may also be administered by using needles which are placed in the prostate and filled, temporarily, with radioactive material like iridium.

Seed implantation is performed with tiny metal capsules, measuring 4.5 mm long and 1 mm wide. These seeds are small enough that they can be lined up inside a thin needle but can be easily seen on X-ray or ultrasound. Iodine-125 is used most commonly since it radiates only a very small area. Tissue more than 1 cm away from the seed does not receive a significant dose.

Iodine-125 has a half life of two months, so that every two months the amount of radiation it gives out is reduced by half. The seeds are not significantly radioactive after a one year period. By placing multiple seeds (between 40 and 100, depending on the size of the prostate), and ensuring that they are very evenly distributed throughout the prostate, the entire prostate gland can be radiated. The rectum (which usually lies more than 1 cm away from the prostate) receives only a low radiation dose. If the cancer has extended through the capsule of the prostate, or if the prostate is very large, seed implantation will not be effective. Brachytherapy is only appropriate for patients who have early, favorable cancer. This means you must have a PSA less than 10; a Gleason score less than 7; either no nodule that can be felt, or a very small one; and a prostate volume less than 50 cc.

There are two steps to the procedure. In a planning session, a trans-rectal ultrasound is used to make serial images of the prostate at 5 mm intervals. This information is then fed into a computer which digitally recreates the prostate and calculates the optimal sites for seed placement. If the prostate is found to be greater than 50 cc, you may be placed on hormone therapy for about 3 months to reduce its size.

The implant itself is carried out under regional (spinal or epidural) anesthesia. The patient is awake, but frozen in the saddle area. A catheter is placed in the bladder. The patient's genitals and perineum (area behind the scrotum) are sterilized before the transrectal ultrasound probe is placed in the rectum. A metal grid is set up in front of the perineum to guide the needles containing the seeds into precise position. Throughout the 90-minute implant process, the seed positions are checked by ultrasound and x-ray. The catheter is removed about an hour after the procedure, and the patient can go home. Your doctor may prescribe an alpha-blocker drug and/or a urinary pain killer like Pyridium to reduce urinating symptoms.

The side effects of brachytherapy include bladder irritation (common), an inability to urinate (fairly uncommon, and usually subsides after a few months), rectal irritation (also fairly uncommon), and loss of erection (occurs in 20-50% of cases).

External beam irradiation

The linear accelerator is a tube into which electrons are injected and accelerated on a radio wave, and then aimed at a target which converts their energy to x-rays or invisible light particles (photons). The energy produced in this way is much higher than the energy produced by cobalt and other isotopes. The higher the energy, the deeper the tissue penetration, allowing for more effective treatment of tumors such as prostate cancer.

Planning is a crucial component of any radiation treatment. Several beams of x-rays are used to give as even a dose as possible across the cancer with the lowest possible dose to surrounding normal structures, especially the rectum and bladder. CT scans are used to delineate the prostate and normal tissues. Lead or lead substitute materials which block x-rays are used to allow the treatment to conform to the shape and volume of the prostate (conformal radiation). Using a computerized guidance system, the beam of radiation is shaped or conformed in three dimensions so that the radiation is confined to the prostate and a 1.5 cm margin around it. The prostate, seminal vesicles, and sometimes the pelvic lymph nodes draining the prostate are included in the field.

The total treatment consists of 30-35 fractions, given once a day, five days a week, for 6-7 weeks. Each treatment consists of a dose of radiation of between 180 to 250 centiGrey (cGy), or rads, directed at the prostate. The total dose should be between 6500 and 7500 cGy. Recent research suggests that a cure is more likely at a dose of at least 7200 cGy, but this higher dose also affects the rectum. At the higher doses, therefore, it is particularly important that the conformal approach is used to reduce the amount of radiation to the rectum.

Practical aspects of radiation therapy

The treatment always begins with simulation—a modified x-ray machine that produces a computerized x-ray of the patient's pelvis, allowing the location of the prostate to be established clearly with respect to the radiation beam. Simulation is required because of variation in the exact location of the prostate from patient to patient. Tattoos are placed on the abdomen so that the position can be easily identified throughout the treatment.

Each treatment takes 10 to 15 minutes, including the positioning and checking. The actual radiation exposure lasts for 2 to 4 minutes. It is completely painless.

The patient will be asked to take off his outer clothing and lie on his back while the machine is set up. It is essential that he be in exactly the same position for each treatment. Some machines use visible laser beams to ensure the patient is perfectly aligned. During treatment, a technologist sits behind a window and watches to make sure there are no problems.

Results of radiation treatment

The likelihood of cure with radiation depends to a large degree on the stage and grade of the cancer at the time of diagnosis. Overall, the chance of being alive ten years after radiation is approximately 70% and the chance of being free of recurrence of prostate cancer, about 60%. The highest likelihood of success occurs when the PSA is less than 15 and the Gleason score less than 7. In favorable cases, chances are considerably better than the numbers above. After radiation, the PSA should fall to low levels, preferably less than 1.0 and, it should remain at a low level. A progressive rise in the PSA means that the cancer will recur eventually, although this may take many years.

Several groups in the U.S. now use a combination of external beam and seed implantation, particularly for more advanced prostate cancer. The attraction of this approach is that a very high dose of radiation can be delivered to the prostate, with a greater chance of cure than either approach alone. The disadvantage is that side effects are greater, particularly with respect to the rectum. At the time of writing, there are very limited long-term follow-up data on the use of the combined approach. If further studies support the long term effectiveness of combined external beam and seeds, this approach may become more popular in the future.

Likelihood of cure with radiation
According to grade, stage, and PSA

PSA	<10	10-20	>20
Gleason 2-6, Stage T1c-T2a	80%	50%	35%
Gleason 7, T1c-T2a	65%	35%	25%
Gleason 8-10, T1c-T2a	40%	25%	20%
Gleason 2-6, T2b-c	70%	40%	35%
Gleason 7, T2b-c	60%	35%	30%
Gleason 8-10 T2b-c	30%	20%	20%
Gleason 2-6, T3	50%	30%	30%
Gleason 7, T3	40%	30%	20%
Gleason 8-10, T3	20%	10%	5%

Side Effects of External Beam Irradiation

There are no side effects of radiation for the first few weeks. As the dose accumulates, however, there is often increasing fatigue. There is also a sensation of rectal discomfort, diarrhea, and an urge to urinate frequently. These symptoms can usually be controlled with medication and generally disappear within two months after stopping treatment. There is a small chance that the patient will be left with permanent radiation injury to the rectum, which may mean diarrhea, blood in the stool, or difficulty controlling the stool.

Radiation reduces erections in about 50% of patients. This occurs gradually over a period of 1-2 years following treatment. The main reason for this is that radiation often produces some narrowing of the blood vessels in the radiated field, and thus the amount of blood flow available to the penis is reduced.

Radiation after Surgery

External beam radiation is used after a prostatectomy when the pathologist reports that the cancer has extended beyond the prostate. It is also used when the PSA starts to rise after surgery. After surgery, the side effects of radiation are quite minor. In a patient with a rising PSA, the chance that the PSA will return to undetectable levels after radiation is about 50%.

CHAPTER ELEVEN

Hormone therapy

Charles Huggins, a Canadian working in the United States, won the Nobel prize for his work on hormone therapy for prostate cancer. In 1941, he found that reducing the levels of male hormones caused regression of prostate cancer. Since that time, continuing work on hormone therapy has resulted in a number of significant advances.

Male hormones fall into two groups. Testosterone, the male hormone present in the largest quantity in the body, is made by the testicles. Smaller amounts of male hormones are made by the adrenal glands. These hormones circulate through the body and pass by diffusion into all cells. Some cells, including prostate cells, both benign and malignant, contain two crucial molecules that are required for the action of these hormones. The first is 5-alpha-reductase. This converts the testosterone to dihydrotestosterone (DHT), a much more powerful hormone.

These hormones in turn bind to the second required molecule, the androgen receptor. This molecule is present only in hormone-dependent cells. The complex of androgen receptor and male hormone then passes inside the cell nucleus, where it binds to the DNA and signals the cell to grow. Thus the male hormones act as signals to the prostate cancer cell to grow. When male hormones are not present, most of the prostate cancer cells stop growing and many of them die.

If that were the whole story, the treatment of prostate cancer would simply consist of reducing male hormone levels. Unfortunately, a small percentage of prostate cancer cells are hormone-resistant—they are able to grow without the hormone signal. The most common reason for this is a mutation or abnormality in the androgen receptor molecule. The mutation allows the cell to grow even when there is no male hormone present. These independent cells begin as a very small proportion of the total prostate cancer cell population, about one in a 100,000. However, they continue to grow over time while the other prostate cancer cells remain stable or decrease in number. Eventually, these hormone-resistant cells become the predominant prostate cancer cells in the patient. This condition is termed hormone-refractory disease and will eventually lead to the patient's death.

Nonetheless, hormone therapy remains effective in dealing with many cases of prostate cancer. Although it may not lead to a cure, it does lengthen life span and keep the disease under control for a considerable period of time.

Side effects

The initial side effects of reducing the level of male hormones are mild. One noticeable effect is a decreased interest in sex, what Freud called libido. With hormone therapy, libido decreases quite rapidly. Eventually, erections are also lost, though these take longer to be affected, and may continue for up to six months or a year after the hormone therapy has begun.

The second early noticeable side effect is hot flashes. These are similar to the flashes that women experience during menopause. They are experienced as a feeling of being hot and then cold, even in neutral temperatures. They are often associated with sweating and can vary from mild to quite severe.

Hot flashes can be easily controlled with a low dose of either estrogen or progesterone-like drugs. These include cyproterone acetate (Androcur), medroxy-progesterone (Megace) or estrogen patches (Estra-derm). If you are experiencing bothersome hot flashes, you should ask your doctor for these remedies.

The more insidious and potentially severe side effects of hormone therapy occur over the long term. Not surprisingly, the loss of male hormones has a feminizing effect on men that goes beyond loss of libido and hot flashes. There is a decrease in muscle mass and a rounding of body shape. Osteoporosis occurs commonly. Personality changes occur gradually over time. Men often notice a decrease in energy, and depression occurs commonly, usually mild. An increase in mood swings is also common, though this effect is more pronounced in some men than in others.

Methods for achieving castrate levels of testosterone

The major goal of hormone therapy for prostate cancer is to reduce the level of testosterone to very low levels, called "castrate levels." A secondary goal, which will be discussed later, is reducing the effect of the other adrenal male hormones. This combination approach is termed total androgen blockade (TAB). Note that the effect on prostate cancer is largely related to the reduction in hormone levels and not to the effect of the drugs themselves on the cancer.

The traditional approach to achieving this is surgical castration. This involves removal of both testicles. The procedure is usually done under local anasthetic with some sedation. It is a minor operation, requiring 20 to 30 minutes, and can usually be done on an outpatient basis.

The advantages of surgical castration are that it is a one-time-only treatment, it effectively achieves the desired goal without any concerns about a patient remaining on a treatment program and has no serious side effects beyond those produced by the absence of the male hormone. The major drawbacks of surgical castration are twofold. First, it has a negative psycho-logical impact that makes it unappealing for many men.

Although the non-surgical approach essentially renders the testicles non-functioning, many men are reluctant to part with their testicles when there is any non-surgical alternative. The second disadvantage is that surgical castration is irreversible and permanent. In contrast, the drugs that are used for prostate cancer can be used short or long term, depending on circumstances. This is particularly relevant with respect to the intermittent hormone therapy approach.

The alternative to surgical castration is medical castration. Male hormones can be reduced using one or a combination of the following four types of drugs.

LHRH analogs

LHRH analogs are now the most common means for achieving castrate levels of testosterone. LHRH is released by the hypothalamus in the brain. It stimulates the pituitary to produce LH, which tells the testicles to make testosterone. LHRH analogs mimic the action of LHRH. Paradoxically, however, after an initial sharp rise in LH, which occurs for about two weeks after an LHRH analog is given, the LH falls to close to zero and stays there as long as the LHRH analog is administered. Similarly, the testosterone rises initially for several weeks and then falls to close to zero. The major drawback of these drugs is that they require administration by injection. They are used in a "depot" or slow-release format that requires repeat injections every or three months. Four-month and even 12-month formulations are being developed but are not yet available.

In Canada, there are three types of LHRH analogs: Lupron, a three-month injection given into the buttock (intramuscularly); Suprefact, a two-month depot given by needle into the abdominal fat (subcutaneous); and Zoladex, a three-month depot given in the same way. Other than the length of time that the drugs last and the place that they are injected, there are no significant differences between them. The side effects of the LHRH analogs, other than those that occur as a result of the low levels of male hormone, are very few. The major one is discomfort at the site of injection, which is usually mild.

Control of testosterone production

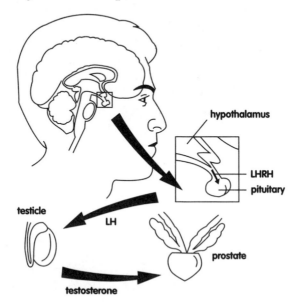

The advantages of the LHRH analogs are that they are safe and free of serious side effects (aside from the effect on testosterone). The disadvantages are that they require periodic injection, that they cause an initial flare effect (the temporary rise in testosterone after the initial injection) and the cost of the drug.

Flare effect

The initial rise in LH and testosterone occur only with the first injection of LHRH analog. After that, testosterone remains suppressed indefinitely as long as the drug is continued. This flare effect is short term and can be blocked by the use of anti-androgens (discussed in the next section). In patients who have very advanced metastatic prostate cancer, particularly when the cancer has spread to the vertebral column and is close to the spinal cord, the rise in testosterone during this flare may cause the hormone-sensitive cancer cells to grow and compress the spinal cord. This may cause paralysis of the legs. The flare effect is rarely a problem if the patients are placed on anti-androgens a few days before the first LHRH injection.

Cost factors

LHRH analogs are extremely expensive. The cost of a single three-month injection is about $1000. In fact, as anti-cancer drugs go, this cost is quite typical. However, because prostate cancer is so common, and because patients with prostate cancer often live for many years with the disease, the total cost of the hormone therapy drugs for prostate cancer has become extremely high. In most provinces in Canada, these drugs are now paid for by the health insurance plan for patients over the age of 65. Whether the drug benefit plans will be able to continue to do this, as the population ages and the number of patients with prostate cancer increases, remains to be seen.

Anti-androgens

For male hormones to signal the cell to grow, they have to bind to the androgen receptor first. Anti-androgens work by binding to the androgen receptors in the cell and blocking the attachment of the DHT to the receptor. This prevents the DHT-receptor complex from acting. Thus these drugs can be used either in combination with castration to block the adrenal hormones from acting, or by themselves.

Cyproterone acetate (Androcur)

This is a drug that acts in two ways. First, it is an anti-androgen, acting to block the androgen receptor. Second, since it is similar in structure to progesterone, a female hormone, cyproterone acts to lower the level of LH and thus testosterone. The major limitation of cyproterone is that the LH suppression is incomplete and diminishes after about a year. When the drug is used by itself, both the LH and testosterone rise to levels above castrate by one year. This effect can be reduced by the addition of a very low dose of estrogen (diethylstil-bestrol, or DES, 0.1 mg per day). The addition of low-dose DES also means that the dose of the cyproterone acetate can be reduced. When used alone, it requires 100 mg three times per day. When used in conjunction with 0.1 mg of DES per day, the dose can be as low as 50 mg three times per day. This combination of low-dose cyproterone acetate and low-dose DES is relatively inexpensive.

Only a few patients report side effects, which consist mainly of an increased risk of blood clot formation. In some rare cases, the drug causes liver damage so patients must be monitored for this. The major concern with a cyproterone regimen is that, unlike the LHRH analogs, cyproterone has never been compared directly to standard therapy (either surgical castration or LHRH analogs).

Non-steroidal anti-androgens

This class of drugs works by binding their molecules to the androgen receptor and preventing male hormones from binding to it. These drugs are "pure" in the sense that they have no effect on LH. In fact, due to a negative feedback effect, the testosterone goes up in patients who are on anti-androgens alone. There are three non-steroidal anti-androgens: flutamide (Euflex), nilutamide (Anandron) and bicalutamide (Casodex). These drugs have been used primarily in combination with LHRH analogs to block the testosterone flare. They have also been used with orchidectomy (surgical castration) and LHRH analogs to produce total androgen blockade.

Total androgen blockade (TAB)

In 1980, Fernand Labrie, a Canadian researcher in Quebec, proposed that prostate cancer in patients progressed in spite of castration because of the presence of androgens produced by the adrenal glands. These adrenal hormones continued to stimulate the prostate in patients who had been castrated. Labrie and others helped to develop the concept of total androgen blockade. This consists of chemical or surgical castration to reduce testosterone and an anti-androgen to block the effect of the adrenal hormones. Labrie's initial study showed huge survival benefits in a small group of patients treated with combination therapy compared to castration alone.

Labrie's initial work lead to a flurry of interest and 27 randomized studies comparing castration to total androgen blockade. These studies have given us conflicting results. Some have shown a significant survival benefit of several years, particularly for patients who have less extensive cancer. Others have shown no benefit whatsoever. The largest trial ever carried out compared surgical castration to castration plus flutamide, but it showed no definite evidence of a benefit of the drug. There was a slight trend to a survival benefit in the combination group but this could have occurred by chance. In addition, there were more side effects from treatment in the total androgen blockade group.

At the moment, TAB is an option for patients since it likely provides a modest survival benefit. The best estimate of this benefit is three months, on average. On the other hand, TAB is associated with increased side effects and increased cost. There remains considerable uncertainty as to whether the modest benefit of this approach reflects the possibility that some patients benefit substantially and many not at all, depending on the extent and site of disease, presence of androgen receptor mutations in the cancer, etc. Some studies have suggested that patients with only a small number of metastases, or no metastases, benefit more substantially from TAB, with a survival benefit of more than two years. The scientific proof of this remains lacking.

Patients choosing hormone therapy should discuss the question of TAB with their doctor. They should be informed that whether they use this approach or not, the impact on the outcome of their disease is likely to be small.

Side effects of non-steroidal anti-androgens

All the anti-androgens can produce liver toxicity. This usually occurs shortly after the drug is started. Patients on these drugs need to have their liver function tests monitored one month after starting treatment, and then annually. The effect is reversible if detected early since stopping the drug will result in return of liver function tests to normal in most cases. Rarely, the drugs cause inflammation of the lungs (interstitial pneumonitis). Patients should also have a chest x-ray annually and be on the alert for increasing shortness of breath.

There are also some specific side effects:

- Flutamide causes diarrhea in 25% of patients. This usually requires stopping the drug.
- Nilutamide causes a decrease in light accommodation. This means that when someone goes from a lighted area into dark (for example, leaving the house to go driving at night) it takes longer for the eyes to adjust to dark. This is rarely a major problem, and can be handled by putting on sunglasses for 10 minutes before going outside at night. It also has a mild "antabuse" effect, meaning that it may cause nausea, headache, and various other symptons with alcohol ingestion. Patients can usually consume small amounts of alcohol without this effect occurring, however.
- Casodex has no specific side effects beyond those mentioned previously.

Anti-androgens as monotherapy

These drugs have been used as monotherapy (single form of treatment), in place of castration. At the doses used for total androgen blockade, the survival of patients treated with anti-androgen alone is worse than that of patients treated with castration. Recent data, however, indicates that high-dose Casodex (150 mg per day) produces comparable survival to castration only in patients who do not have metastatic disease. In patients with metastatic disease the survival is inferior even with high doses of Casodex. The advantage of monotherapy is that some side effects of treatment, particularly impotence, are reduced. For patients who are anxious to preserve sexual function, this may be a reasonable option. High-dose Casodex is not yet available in Canada, though may be approved by the time you read this.

The other problem with monotherapy with the non-steroidal anti-androgens is breast enlargement (gynecomastia). When these drugs are used alone, the hypothalamus "sees" a lower level of androgen. The result is an increase in LHRH, LH and testosterone. This higher level of testosterone is blocked by the anti-androgen in the prostate. However, tissues elsewhere in the body, particularly the skin, convert testosterone to estrogen so the levels of estrogen in the body rise, producing breast enlargement. This can be very troublesome for men on monotherapy. The breast enlargement can be prevented by a low dose of radiation to the breasts prior to starting treatment. Once gynecomastia has occurred, however, it is relatively permanent even if the drug is stopped. In patients on combination therapy, because the testosterone remains low, there is no increased conversion to estrogens and, therefore, gynecomastia should not occur.

Other hormonal agents

Diethylstilbestrol (DES), a form of estrogen, was the standard therapy for advanced prostate cancer between

1940 and 1985. This drug effectively produces castrate levels of testosterone. However, it is associated with a substantially increased risk of blood-clot formation (thromboembolic events). These clots may occur in the legs, producing deep vein thrombosis or pulmonary embolism; in the heart, producing a heart attack; or in the brain, producing a stroke. Of patients put on DES, 10 to 30% will have such an event. Recent attempts to reduce the risk of blood-clot formation using a blood thinner do not seem to make a difference. Although very inexpensive, DES has been largely abandoned as a monotherapy. It is still used at a very low dose in combination with cyproterone acetate (Androcur). At that dose, the risk of blood clots is small.

Intermittent therapy

Historically, patients going on hormone therapy for advanced prostate cancer remained on treatment for life. In the pre-PSA era (until 1989), patients were usually started on hormone treatment when they had a spread of prostate cancer to the bones. These patients lived an average of three years from the time of treatment. In most cases they died of prostate cancer before they experienced the long-term side effects of hormone therapy, side effects that include osteoporosis, muscle loss and personality changes.

Since the advent of PSA, however, the situation has changed dramatically. Patients are now diagnosed earlier, treated with radiation or surgery and started on hormone therapy when their PSA begins to climb. Often the patient has no evidence of recurrent prostate cancer other than a rising PSA. These patients have a very long life expectancy, in the neighborhood of 10 to 15 years, though it depends on other factors including grade, PSA prior to treatment and extent of the cancer. Since the average survival of these patients is much longer than it was when patients were treated when the disease had spread to the bone, they are at much more risk for the development of the side effects of hormone therapy. For many patients who are over 75 or have other illnesses, the risk of death from other causes is higher than the risk of dying of prostate cancer. For these patients, the quality of life is paramount.

The concept of intermittent hormonal therapy was first proposed in 1986. This involves treating patients for a period of time, usually eight months to a year, then discontinuing therapy. The PSA falls to undetectable levels in most of these patients on treatment. After eight months on treatment, it takes an average of eight months for the PSA to recover. At that point, hormone therapy is restarted. Interestingly, some patients take one to two years before their PSA recovers. In most patients, testosterone recovers promptly after hormone treatment is discontinued. Thus, the patients have a return of their quality of life to the way it was prior to hormone treatment, including return of sexual function. For this reason, the intermittent approach is very attractive to many patients.

The major downside is that the effect of intermittent therapy on survival is unknown. There is some evidence from laboratory models to suggest that there may be a benefit to intermittent therapy. According to these models, the hormone-resistant cells return to a more normal behavior and appearance when re-exposed to male hormones. There is evidence that this occurs, at least in mice. Whether this benefit of intermittent therapy occurs in humans is not known. There are also concerns that the unstable hormonal milieu induced by intermittent hormone treatment may have a negative effect. This question is now being studied in a large clinical trial. The answer as to whether intermittent therapy improves or reduces survival should be known around the year 2008. In the meantime, it seems reasonable for older patients, or patients who are very concerned about the loss of sexual function that goes along with hormone therapy, to stop their treatment after they have been on it for a year or so. Such patients need to have their PSA and testosterone monitored every two months. When the PSA returns to the level it was before therapy was started, hormone treatment should be restarted. Over the course of a decade, these patients are likely to be on and off treatment four to six times.

At this point, intermittent therapy should be considered experimental. Patients taking this approach must understand this and realize that intermittent therapy may be associated with a slight decrease in survival.

Indications for hormone therapy

Hormone therapy is clearly warranted for patients who have metastatic prostate cancer, in lymph nodes, bones or elsewhere. It is also indicated for patients who have very advanced local disease, that is, where the prostate cancer has spread well beyond the prostate out to the side walls of the body.

Hormone therapy is also indicated for patients who've had radical treatment, particularly radiation, in whom the PSA subsequently starts to rise. Two successive rises in PSA, even if this occurs at a low level, almost always means that the prostate cancer has recurred. At this point, however, we do not know how high the PSA should be before hormone therapy is started. Waiting until the disease has spread to the bones may be too late and definitely reduces survival and life expectancy. However, there are no studies showing what the PSA trigger point should be. Treatment when the PSA just begins to rise (from 0.5 to 1 ng/mL) is too early. The prostate cancer may be slow growing and still pose no threat to the patient. Long-term hormone therapy does pose a threat to your quality of life.

Therefore, we should wait until the PSA shows signs of a steady rise, and an absolute PSA of at least 6 before therapy is started. If the PSA is rising slowly, waiting until it has reached 20 is perfectly reasonable and will reduce the side effects and costs of treatment.

Neoadjuvant therapy

"Adjuvant" treatment means therapy given in addition to or as an adjunct to more definitive treatment. Neoadjuvant therapy is given before the definitive treatment and adjuvant therapy given afterwards. It can boost the effect of the main treatment, or reduce symptoms or have a combination of benefits for patients in treatment.

The use of hormones before surgery clearly shrinks the cancer and reduces the likelihood of a positive surgical margin. This observation, made in the mid-90s, led to tremendous enthusiasm for neoadjuvant therapy before surgery. However, follow-up studies on these patients show that three months of hormones prior to surgery has absolutely no impact on the likelihood of cure. In fact, it may even have a negative effect. At this time, neoadjuvant hormones prior to surgery have been abandoned. It is possible that a longer period of hormone therapy before surgery might have some benefit and this is now the subject of clinical trials. In general, patients should not take hormones before radical prostatectomy.

In contrast to the situation with surgery, hormones before radiation treatment *have* been associated with an increased likelihood of response and increased likelihood of cure. The difference between the effect of hormones before surgery and radiation probably relates to the fact that radiation response is dependent on the volume of the cancer in a way that surgery is not.

Reducing the volume of the cancer increases the likelihood of cure in a patient treated with radiation. Hormones before radiation are worthwhile in patients who have bulky or advanced prostate cancer and improve the likelihood of response by 15 to 20%.

Hormones have also been used as a follow-up to radiation treatment. One study showed that using hormones for three years after radiation treatment improved the survival by 22%. Thus, patients with advanced local disease are usually treated with both neoadjuvant therapy (for three months) and adjuvant therapy (for two to three years after treatment). For patients with early disease (patients who are candidates for brachytherapy), there is no evidence that the hormone treatment makes a difference.

DRUGS FOR PROSTATE DISEASES

DRUG TYPE	BRAND NAMES	GENERIC NAMES
Steroidal anti-androgens:	Androcur	cyproterone
	Megace	medroxyprogesterone
Nonsteroidal anti-androgens:	Anandron	nilutamide
	Casodex	bicalutamide
	Euflex	flutamide
Estrogens:	DES	diethylstilbestrol
	Estraderm	estrogen patch
LHRH analogs:	Lupron	leuprolide
	Suprefact	buserelin
	Zoladex	goserelin
Chemotherapeutic drugs:	Emcyt	estramustine
	Etoposide	etoposide
	Novantrone	mitoxantrone
Drugs to improve potency:	Caverject	alprostadil
	Muse	alprostadil
	Viagra	sildenafil
Drugs to improve urination:	Cardura	doxazosyn
	Flomax	tamsulosin
	Hytrin	terazosin
	Proscar	finasteride
	Ultimate Balance Pro	saw palmetto

CHAPTER TWELVE

Management of hormone refractory prostate cancer

The limitation of hormone therapy reflects the fact that the cancers eventually become populated by cells that no longer respond to the absence of male hormones. Although hormone treatment is far and away the most effective therapy for prostate cancer, once hormone refractory (resistant) disease is present, there is no treatment that has been shown to improve survival. However, there are a number of therapies for hormone refractory disease that offer some improvement in quality of life.

The most important treatment for hormone refractory disease is spot radiation. Patients frequently have painful prostate cancer in the bone, and 70% of such men respond well to a one- to three-day course of radiation. This is very effective for patients who have only a few painful sites. There are no side effects of radiation when it is used in this fashion.

Modification of hormones sometimes produces a favorable response. The anti-androgens may become stimulatory later in the disease as the androgen receptor undergoes further mutations. Thus, the first step in a patient whose PSA is rising in spite of low levels of testosterone, is to discontinue the anti-androgen. There have also been some successes in switching from one anti-androgen to another. For example, patients who have been treated with flutamide should have the treatment stopped, wait for their PSA to begin rising again and then be placed on bicalutimide. Such patients often demonstrate a good response, although it is usually short lived (about three months).

For patients who are more symptomatic, with multiple painful areas, or who are generally feeling unwell due to cancer progression, chemotherapy may be used. The most effective regimen to date is the combination of mitoxantrone plus prednisone. This has been shown to result in an improvement of quality of life (but no improvement in survival). The side effects of mitoxantrone are minimal. Prednisone produces an improvement in appetite, mood and sense of well-being. The response to these agents is usually only a few months, and they produce no survival benefit.

Another combination of drugs for hormone refractory disease is estramustine (Emcyt) and VP16 (Etoposide). Emcyt is both a female hormone and a chemotherapeutic agent (nitrogen mustard). Etoposide is a chemotherapeutic agent. Both these drugs interfere with cell division. In contrast to mitoxantrone and prednisone, this combination has quite substantial side effects, including nausea and vomiting, fatigue and fluid retention. Although it has been shown to produce a PSA response in about 50% of patients, this is usually short lived. There is no evidence of a survival benefit with this regimen.

Strontium, prednisone and experimental treatments

Strontium is a radioactive molecule that concentrates in bone. When injected systemically, it is taken up by bone where the radiation can result in shrinkage of the painful metastatic sites. This drug reduces pain in patients who have many painful metastases in bone but there is no survival benefit. The major limitations are that it causes anemia by suppressing red cell formation and is relatively costly.

Prednisone is often used alone. It produces a fall in PSA in about a quarter of patients and produces a short-term improvement in well-being.

There are a number of experimental regimens around North America using new agents to treat advanced prostate cancer. Gene therapy is also being studied. To date, however, none of these drugs have shown any evidence of a survival benefit. Patients who are interested should be encouraged to seek out therapeutic trials of new agents for hormone refractory disease. However, until there is evidence of survival benefit from one of these new agents, you should be cautioned against expending substantial time, effort or money in the pursuit of these treatments. There is a pressing need for improved therapies for hormone refractory disease, but we do not have these at the present time. What is important is that a patient's quality of life be maximized.

ALTERNATIVE/COMPLEMENTARY THERAPIES

The term "complementary therapy" is usually used for treatments such as massage, tai chi relaxation techniques,and the similar exercises that work along with regular medical treatment. The name alternative therapy" is generally used to describe treatments based on naturopathy, homeopathy and related fields whose medical effects are still unproven.

Complementary therapies that help you to feel more relaxed, stronger and more in control of your life are helpful and safe. Although alternative medicine clearly helps some people to feel better, you must always be careful when such treatments involve prescription of herbs or other "natural" products.

It is important to realize that highly touted herbal drugs are simply drugs that come from plants, as do many prescribed medications. Digoxin, the heart medication, comes from the foxglove plant; taxol, a very valuable drug for ovarian cancer, comes from the Pacific yew tree; vincristine, a drug for leukemia, comes from the vinca plant; and aspirin was originally an extract of willow bark. In other words, there is nothing exclusive to "alternative therapy" about the use of medicines derived from plants.

But there are important differences between most herbal products and conventional drugs derived from plants. The conventional drugs are purified and carefully studied before being approved by our regulatory agencies for use. Side effect profiles are established by initial research. Because we know that new side effects, undetected during pre-market testing, can still arise, there are ongoing surveillance and reporting mechanisms in place to track new issues related to a particular prescribed medications. This arrangement is not perfect, but the desire for absolute safety must be balanced by the need for new, improved treatments for many diseases.

The problems with most herbal products begin with these: 1) You don't know if what's on the label is what's in the bottle and 2) You don't know if what's in the bottle is pure. A few years ago, kelp products were popular as an alternative medicine. Some of these products turned out to contain significant amounts of arsenic, and there were several cases of arsenic poisoning. Among other risks, liver cancer can result from excessive intake of arsenic.

In dealing with alternative medicine, the most important issue is that of safety. You should always assume that anything that can have benefit for you might also have risks and side effects. Because there is no government regulation in place for alternative medicines requiring the makers of herbal products to test their products scientifically, we simply don't know the risks in taking most herbal products. This does not mean that such products won't help some people; it's just that you can't assume they are "safe" just because someone tells you that they are. Over the years, there have been many herbal products that have been intentionally taken off the market after serious and sometimes fatal side effects were discovered.

Fortunately, there are some herbal products that have been studied for certain forms of prostate disease that are useful, and relatively safe. The best known is saw palmetto (see pages 11 and 12). Evening primrose oil is sometimes used to reduce hot flashes in men on androgen ablation therapy (see page 95). The likely reason for this use is that this oil contains phytoestrogens (plant-based estrogens).

Pain control

Effective pain control is crucial for patients with hormone refractory disease and can usually be accomplished with minimal sedation. The three components of effective pain control are:

1. use of long-acting morphine or related drugs to prevent painful episodes
2. use of shorter-acting breakthrough medications (Acetaminophen with Codeine) for breakthrough pain
3. routine treatment of constipation with laxatives and stool softeners

Thus, a typical patient with hormone refractory prostate cancer and bone metastases who is experiencing moderately severe pain might be on long-acting morphine, 15 to 60 mg every eight to 12 hours; a nonsteroidal anti-inflammatory like ibuprofen; Percocet 2-4 tablets every four hours for breakthrough pain; a stool softener; and powerful laxatives. These drugs can offer dramatic improvement in the quality of life for a patient who is in pain.

Emergencies

The most important emergency facing a patient with hormone refractory prostate cancer is cord compression. This occurs if a vertebral metastasis compresses the spinal cord. Patients who have known large vertebral metastases or back pain from metastatic disease are at risk for cord compression. Although these patients often have back pain beforehand, the pain may be minor. When cord compression does occur, it will be extremely painful and serious. Patients can be treated either with radiation to the area or with surgical decompression. This is an emergency and treatment needs to be initiated within hours. Even when it is, some patients will not recover use of their legs.

A second problem is urinary retention (inability to urinate) or bleeding through the penis from locally advanced prostate cancer. This is usually managed with transurethral resection of the obstructing or bleeding tissue. Radiation is also used if the prostate has not been previously radiated.

CHAPTER THIRTEEN

Living with a cancer diagnosis

Cancer affects the mind as well as the body. Being given a diagnosis of cancer creates a sense of isolation and a wide range of conflicting emotions. Patients feel an overriding sense of uncertainty about their future. This is colored by polarities of despair and hope, fear and confidence, anger and humor. People cope in a wide variety of ways.

Many patients go through a series of stages as they come to terms with the diagnosis. This is similar to the process of grief associated with the loss of a close family member. The initial reaction is often one of disbelief that the diagnosis is correct. This is part of the feeling of denial of the situation. Patients often feel angry, asking "Why me?" Eventually, most patients accept that the diagnosis is correct, that they do in fact have prostate cancer. This acceptance allows patients to adjust to the implications of a diagnosis of cancer. The disbelief-denial-anger-acceptance process is healthy as long as it doesn't interfere with a patient seeking appropriate treatment.

Patients use a variety of techniques to help them cope with the cancer. Here are four of the most important.

Sharing information with family and friends

It is difficult to keep information about cancer from family and close friends. In most situations, sharing information about the disease helps you to cope with it and allows your family to give you support and help. A blanket approach is not necessarily the best, however. It may be appropriate for you to spare the details from family members who are too young, too old or too fragile.

It is also a mistake for family members to hide a diagnosis from the patient. In most cases, patients are better off knowing the diagnosis and the likely outcomes. Otherwise, the patient becomes isolated from the family and relationships become strained and false. The patient may end up feeling resentful and hurt. Almost all men can eventually come to terms with the diagnosis of prostate cancer. Sharing the experience with family members is important.

You should also bring your children into the picture. Openness about the situation gives them a chance to talk about it, ask questions and express their feelings. If the disease results in significant family disruption, it is particularly important that children understand the cause so that they don't feel responsible themselves.

Support groups

Many prostate cancer support groups exist across Canada. These are formed by patients with prostate cancer and supported by professionals in the area. Meetings of the support groups provide an opportunity for patients to share their experience of the disease. It is very comforting to discuss your experiences with others who have gone through the same process. Often members of the group have ideas and suggestions that are helpful. Membership in support groups can also give you a sense of control and empowerment as well as the satisfaction of helping others. A list of support groups is provided in Appendix 2.

A support group will help you relate to your doctors and other members of the health-care team as an active participant, not a passive patient. They will show you how to identify one team member who will serve as the quarterback or leader. This may be your family doctor, urologist or oncologist. This person needs to be someone who is available regularly and helps guide you through the health-care system. You must be prepared to participate in decision making.

Changing doctors

Managing your prostate cancer can be challenging for both yourself and your doctor. Good communication is vital, but sometimes this communication is lacking. A few doctors lack communication skills; some lack empathy; some seem too pressed for time.

Sometimes, you may not "click" with your doctor. If you feel that this is the case, or that you have lost confidence in your doctor, you're entitled to change. Usually, your family doctor can refer you to someone else. A change should not be made lightly, however. Often, mentioning your dissatisfaction to your caregiver may be enough to improve his or her behavior. It is also worth remembering that doctors are human beings, not saints. No doctor can promise you heaven on earth.

Optimism is the key

It is essential to maintain hope. Hope gives you the psychological strength to carry on and cope with the demands of diagnosis and treatment. Hope needs to be nurtured. It is based on the idea that things may improve in spite of the current situation. Family members can help nurture hope by assisting you in having realistic goals and by providing love and support.

CHAPTER FOURTEEN

Research and the future

Unfortunately, research into prostate cancer was neglected until recently due to inadequate funding. In Canada, breast cancer, which affects the same number of patients and causes the same number of deaths per year, has received 35 times as much funding in the last few years as prostate cancer. But this situation is changing. Governments have recognized that research into the cause, cure and prevention of prostate cancer is a major priority and have provided new sources of funding. New foundations (in Canada, the Canadian Prostate Cancer Research Foundation, and in the United States, CAPCURE) have emerged to assist in the funding of these research initiatives.

This research is very likely to improve the management of the disease in a variety of ways. Improvements will likely come in the following areas:

Prevention An optimal regimen of prevention will be identified using combinations of diet, micronutrients and vitamins.

Screening The degree to which screening reduces the likelihood of dying of prostate cancer will be clearly established.

Molecular markers It should be possible to predict accurately, based on the molecular pattern of the cancer, which cancers pose a threat to the patient and require aggressive treatment and which can be managed conservatively.

Genetic analysis This will the identify the genes involved in the development and progression of prostate cancer, and the patients who are at high risk for the disease, particularly in families with a strong history of prostate cancer.

Combination therapy Certain combinations of different therapies used together will be demonstrated to improve the outcome of treatment. Possible examples include hormone therapy and/or radiation after surgery; harvesting of prostate cancer tissue surgically with subsequent gene therapy; combinations of radiation, microwave thermotherapy and hormone therapy.

Gene therapy The use of artificially constructed genes directed against specific targets promises to revolutionize cancer therapy.

Better therapies for hormone-resistant cancer This may include new chemotherapeutic agents, gene therapies, differentiation inducers, etc.

The field will certainly be very different in 10 to 20 years than it is now. Treatments will be more effective and have fewer side effects. Surgery will be used as much to harvest tissue for gene therapy as for cure. More patients will be cured and will pay a smaller price for it (in terms of side effects). Patients who are not cured will be able to access effective gene-based therapies. Preventive measures will reduce the number of patients diagnosed and dying from the disease.

Acknowledgments

The author wishes to acknowledge the editorial assistance of Dr. Fred Saibil, the assistance of Ms Michelle Skerratt who was invaluable in the preparation of the book, and Dr. Juanita Crook who reviewed the manuscript.

Web sites and other information
Online addresses

www.canadian-prostate.com
- Canadian Prostate Health Council

www.cua.org
- Canadian Urology Association

is.dal.ca/-bellurol/cuog.html
- Canadian Urologic Oncology Group (CUOG)

www.ipguide.com
- Intelligent Patient Guide

www.yahoo.com/health/men's_health
- Men's Health

www.ncc.go.jp
- NCI Cancerfacts

oncolink.upenn.edu/disease/prostate
- Prostate Cancer

www.prostate.org
- Prostatitis Homepage

www.comed.com/prostate
- The Prostate Cancer InfoLink

www.ubc-prostate.com
- UBC Prostate Clinic

www.urologychannel.com
- The Urology Channel

Service organizations and support groups

Canadian Cancer Society

The Canadian Cancer Society is a voluntary organization that provides information, assistance and direction for patients with cancer. The society's goal is to optimize the quality of life of patients and their families by means of a wide variety of social, emotional and psychological support programs.

NATIONAL OFFICE
77 Bloor St. W., Suite 1702
Toronto, ON M5S 5A1
(416) 961-7223

BRITISH COLUMBIA AND YUKON
565 West 10th Ave.
Vancouver, BC V5Z 4J4
(604) 872-4400

ALBERTA AND NORTHWEST TERRITORIES
2424 4th St. SW, Suite 200
Calgary, AB T2S 2T4
(403) 228-4487

SASKATCHEWAN
2445 – 13th Ave., Suite 201
Regina, SK S4P 0Wl
(306) 757-4260

MANITOBA
193 Sherbrook St.
Winnipeg, MB R3C 2B7
(204) 774-7483

ONTARIO
1639 Yonge St.
Toronto, ON M4T 2W6
(416) 488-5400

QUEBEC
5151, boul. de l'Assomption,
Montreal, PQ H1T 4A9
(514) 255-5151

NEW BRUNSWICK
P.O. Box 2089
Saint John, NB E2I 3T5
(506) 634-3180

PRINCE EDWARD ISLAND
1 Rochford St., Suite 1
Charlottetown, PE C1A 9L2
(902) 566-4007

NOVA SCOTIA
201 Roy Building
1657 Barrington St.
Halifax, NS B3J 2A1
(902) 423-6183

NEWFOUNDLAND AND LABRADOR
P.O. Box 8921
St. John's, NF A1B 3R9
(709) 753-6520

Prostate Cancer Research Foundation of Canada
1262 Don Mills Rd., Suite 1F
Don Mills, ON M3B 2W7
This national organization is dedicated to raising funds to support research directed at the cause, prevention and cure of prostate cancer.

International Support Groups

Us Too International
930 North York Rd., Suite 50
Hinsdale, IL 60521-2993
1-800-808-7866

Canadian Prostate Cancer
Support Network
(613) 745-6466

Man To Man
American Cancer Society
1599 Clifton Rd. NE
Atlanta, GA 30329-4251
1-800-ACS-2345

Canadian Support Groups
(from the Westcoast to the East)

BRITISH COLUMBIA

Campbell River Prostate
Support and Awareness Group
(250) 923-1357

Comox Valley Prostate
Support and Awareness Group
(250) 338-8011

Cowichan Valley Prostate
Support and Awareness Group
(250) 743-2046

Prince George Prostate
Support Group
(250) 563-0095

Surrey Prostate Cancer
Support Group
(604) 599-0216

North Shore Prostate Support and Awareness Group
(604) 924-0776

Vancouver Prostate Support and Awareness Group
(604) 434-2100

Victoria Prostate Support and Awareness Group
(250) 474-3860

ALBERTA

Edmonton Us Too
(780) 435-0232

Calgary Us Too
(780) 205-3966

Lethbridge Prostate Cancer
Support Group
(403) 381-2876

Medicine Hat Prostate
Support Group
(403) 529-0617

SASKATCHEWAN

Moose Jaw Us Too
(306) 693-2312

North Battleford Support Group
(306) 445-5237

The Regina Support Group
(306) 766-2248

Saskatoon Us Too
(306) 382-4236

The Yorkton Support Group
(306) 783-3927

MANITOBA

Winnipeg Us Too
(204) 257-6453

ONTARIO

Oshawa Us Too
(905) 579-1980

Mississauga Prostate Cancer
Support Group
(905) 277-3939

Metro Toronto Man To Man
(416) 932-8820

The Lindsay Area Support
Group
(705) 324-5234

Thunder Bay Us Too
(807) 622-9669

Guelph-Wellington Support Group
Canadian Cancer Society
(519) 824-4261

Kingston Support Group
(613) 544-1307

Brantford Support Group
(519) 753-8641

London Prostate Cancer
Information and Support Group
(519) 685-8657

Newmarket Us Too
(905) 853-2665

Ottawa Prostate Support Group
(613) 569-6804

Quinte Prostate Cancer
Support Group
(613) 968-5362

HopeSpring Prostate Cancer
Support Group
(519) 742-4673

Us Too Peterborough
and District Prostate Cancer
Survivor Support Group
(705) 652-6192

North Bay Living with Cancer
Support Group for Men
(705) 472-5253

Brampton Prostate Cancer
Support Group/Us Too
(905) 877-8092

St. Catharines Living with
Prostate Cancer Support Group
(905) 684-6455

QUEBEC

Prostate Cancer Support Group of the Jewish
General Hospital
(514) 340-7558

Canadian Prostate
Cancer Network
Montreal West Island Group
(514) 694-6412

NEW BRUNSWICK

St. John Us Too
(506) 433-1917

Chatham Prostate
Cancer Support Group
(506) 773-3261

NOVA SCOTIA

Cape Breton Prostate
Cancer Support Group
(902) 794-7921

Halifax Prostate Cancer
Information and Support Group
(902) 584-3105

PRINCE EDWARD ISLAND

P.E.I. Prostate Cancer Support Group
(902) 566-4007

Cancer treatment centers

Cancer centers provide chemotherapy and radiation treatment, as well as information and support programs for their patients. Although you cannot simply walk in and ask for treatment unless you live in the area, these centers can offer further information and provide contacts that would be useful for you.

BRITISH COLUMBIA

Vancouver Cancer Centre
600 West 10 Ave.
Vancouver, BC V5Z 4E6
(604) 877-6000

Vancouver Island Cancer Centre
1900 Fort St.
Victoria, BC V8R 1J8
(250) 595-9228

Fraser Valley Cancer Centre
13750-96 Ave.
Surrey, BC V3V 1Z2
(604) 930-2098

ALBERTA

Alberta Cancer Board
6th Fl., 9707-110 St.
Edmonton, AB T5K 2L9
(403) 482-9328

Cross Cancer Institute
11560 University Ave.
Edmonton, AB T6G 1Z2
(780) 492-8771

Grande Prairie Cancer Centre
10409-98 St.
Grande Prairie, AB T8V 2F8
(780) 738-7588

Central Alberta Cancer Centre
3942 -SOA Ave.,
P.O. Bag 5030
Red Deer, AB T4N 6R2
(403) 343-6660

Tom Baker Cancer Centre
1331-29 St. NW
Calgary, AB T2N 4N2
(403) 670-1711

Lethbridge Cancer Clinic
960-19 Street S.
Lethbridge, AB T1J 1W5
(403) 329-0633

Medicine Hat Cancer Centre
666-5th St. SW
Medicine Hat, AB T1A 4H6
(403) 529-8817

SASKATCHEWAN

Saskatchewan Cancer Foundation
Suite 400, 2631-28th Ave.
Regina, SK S4S 6X3
(306) 585-1831

Saskatoon Cancer Centre
20 Campus Dr.
Saskatoon, SK S7N 4H4
(306) 244-4389

Allan Blair Cancer Centre
4101 Dewdney Ave.
Regina, SK S4T 7T1
(306) 359-2643

MANITOBA

Manitoba Cancer Treatment
and Research Foundation
100 Olivia St.
Winnipeg, MB R3E 0V9
(204) 787-2241

ONTARIO

The Ontario Cancer and
Treatment Foundation
(Head Office)
620 University Ave.
Toronto, ON M5G 2L7
(416) 971-9800

The Ontario Cancer Foundation
Hamilton Centre
699 Concession St.
Hamilton, ON L8V 5C2
(905) 527-5949

The Ontario Cancer Foundation
Kingston Centre
25 King St. W.
Kingston, ON K7L 5P9
(613) 544-2630

The Ontario Cancer Foundation
London Centre
790 Commissioners Rd. E.
London, ON N6A 4L6
(519) 685-8600

The Ontario Cancer Foundation
North Eastern Ontario Centre
41 Ramsey Lake Rd.
Sudbury, ON P3E 5J1
(705) 522-6237

The Ontario Cancer Foundation
Ottawa Centre—Civic Hospital Division
190 Melrose Ave.
Ottawa, ON K1Y 4K7
(613) 725-6300

The Ontario Cancer Foundation
Ottawa Centre—General Hospital Division
501 Smyth Rd.
Ottawa, ON KIH 8L6
(613) 725-6300

The Ontario Cancer Foundation
Thunder Bay Centre
290 Munro St.
Thunder Bay, ON P7A 7T1
(807) 343-1610

The Ontario Cancer Foundation
Toronto-Sunnybrook Regional Cancer Centre
2075 Bayview Ave.
North York, ON M4N 3M5
(416) 488-5801

The Ontario Cancer Foundation
Windsor Centre
2220 Kildare Rd.
Windsor, ON N8W 2X3
(519) 253-5253

The Ontario Cancer Institute
Princess Margaret Hospital
610 University Ave.
Toronto, ON M5G 2M9
(416) 924-0671

QUEBEC

The treatment of cancer by radiation in the province of Quebec is undertaken in hospitals with qualified radiation therapists, such as:

Centre hopitalier universitaire de Sherbrooke
3001 nord, 12 av.
Sherbrooke, PQ J1H 5N4
(819) 566-5555

Hôpital Hôtel-Dieu de Chicoutimi
av. St-Vallier
C.P. 1006
Chicoutimi, PQ G7H 5H6
(418) 549-2195

Hôpital Hôtel-Dieu de Montreal
3840, rue St-Urbain
Montreal, PQ H2W 1T8
(514) 843-2611

Hôpital Hôtel-Dieu de Quebec
11, côte du Palais
Quebec, PQ GIR 2J6
(418) 691-5151

Hôpital Maisonneuve-Rosemont
5415, boul. de l'Assomption
Montreal, PQ HIT 2M4
(514) 252-3400

Hôpital Notre-Dame
1560 est, rue Sherbrooke
Montreal, PQ H2L 4K8
(514) 876-6421

Montreal General Hospital
1650 Cedar Ave.
Montreal, PQ H3G 1A4
(514) 937-6011

Montreal Jewish General Hospital
3755 côte Ste-Catherine
Montreal, PQ H3T 1E2
(514) 340-8222

Royal Victoria Hospital
687 Pine Ave. W.
Montreal, PQ H3A IA1
(514) 842-1231

NEW BRUNSWICK

Department of Oncology
Saint John Regional Hospital
P.O. Box 2100
Saint John, NB E2L 4L2
(506) 648-6000

NOVA SCOTIA

The Cancer Treatment and Research Foundation of
Nova Scotia
(Head Office)
5820 University Ave.
Halifax, NS B3H 1V7
(902) 428-4011

Nova Scotia Cancer Centre
5820 University Ave.
Halifax, NS B3H 1V7
(902) 428-4200

PRINCE EDWARD ISLAND

Oncology Clinic, Queen Elizabeth Hospital
Box 6600
Charlottetown, PE CIA 8T5
(902) 894-2027

NEWFOUNDLAND

The Newfoundland Cancer Treatment and Reearch
Foundation,
Dr. H. Bliss Murphy Cancer Centre
300 Prince Philip Dr.
St. John's, NF A1B 3V6
(709) 737-4235

UNITED STATES

American Foundation for Urologic Disease
300 West Pratt St.
Baltimore, MD 21201-2463
(410) 727-2908
1-800-242-2383

Cancer Care, Inc.
1180 Avenue of the Americas
New York, NY 10036
(212) 221-3300

National Kidney and Urologic Diseases
Information Clearing House
Box NKUO1C
9000 Rockville Pike
Bethesda, MD 20892
(301) 654-4415

Glossary

ADENOCARCINOMA The most common type of cancer. The term "adeno" refers to cancers that arise from tissues that are glandular (that secrete substances of some type).

ADJUVANT THERAPY The use of A treatment (radiation, hormone therapy, chemotherapy) in addition to definitive primary treatment. For example, radiation may be used after surgery, or hormone therapy following radiation. Neoadjuvant therapy refers to the use of these additional treatments before the definitive treatment.

ANALGESIC Painkillers such as acetaminophen with codeine.

ANDROGENS Hormones based on the steroid structure, secreted by the testicles and adrenal glands that are responsible for male sexual characteristics.

ANDROGEN ABLATION The removal of testosterone either with drugs or castration.

ANTI-ANDROGENS Drugs used to block the androgens from binding to the androgen receptor, thereby blocking their ability to stimulate prostate cells.

ATELECTASIS Areas of the lung that have collapsed. This can occur after anesthesia.

ATYPIA Cells that appear mildly abnormal but not fully cancerous.

AUTOLOGOUS BLOOD The donation of a patient's own blood up to one month prior to surgery to be used during and after surgery as transfusion, if necessary.

BENIGN PROSTATIC HYPERPLASIA Progressive enlargement and growth of the prostate that occurs in all men, beginning about age 40. The most common cause of urination symptoms.

BIOPSY Removal of tissue for microscopic evaluation to determine the nature of the disease process.

BRACHYTHERAPY The implantation of radioactive material into cancerous tissue. In the prostate this is done either with permanent seeds filled with iodine or palladium, or short-term tubes containing iridium.

CANCER The uncontrolled and unrestricted growth of cells that no longer respond to growth regulatory signals.

CARCINOMA Refers to most cancers, except for those that arise primarily from connective tissue like bone (these are called sarcomas).

CASTRATION Removal of the testicles. Also known as orchidectomy.

CHEMOTHERAPY The treatment of cancer with drugs.

COMPLETE RESPONSE Complete disappearance of all detectable cancer.

CYROSURGERY Using freezing to destroy cancer cells.

CYSTOSCOPY The insertion of a scope (cystoscope) through the urethra and prostate and into the bladder, allowing direct visualization.

DIGITAL-RECTAL EXAMINATION The examination of the prostate by a finger placed through the anus. The prostate can be felt through the wall of the rectum.

DIHYDROTESTOSTERONE The most active and potent androgen, which is produced inside the cell from testosterone by 5-alpha-reductase.

ESTROGEN A female hormone.

5-ALPHA-REDUCTASE The enzyme in androgen-sensitive cells that converts testosterone to the active hormone dihydrotestosterone.

GRADE The degree to which cancer cells look abnormal microscopically. High-grade cells are more abnormal looking and tend to be more aggressive.

GLEASON SCORE The most widely used grading system. It is based on a low-power microscopic view of the cells, and consists of the two most predominant patterns, each graded out of 5, added for a score out of 10.

HEMATURIA Blood in the urine.

INTRAVENOUS PYELOGRAM (IVP) X-rays of the kidneys taken after dye is injected intravenously, to evaluate the structure and function of the kidneys, ureters and bladder.

LAPAROSCOPY Surgery performed through tiny incisions in the abdominal wall through which small tubes are placed. These allow small instruments to be inserted in the abdomen, permitting surgery to be performed with more rapid recovery.

LIBIDO Interest in sex.

LHRH The hormone secreted by the hypothalamus that regulates the level of LH (secreted by the pituitary) and testosterone.

LHRH AGONIST Drugs that mimic the effect of LHRH and paradoxically result in low levels of LH and testosterone.

LYMPH NODES Small structures about the size and shape of lima beans, which are present throughout the body. These act as filters to defend against infections. Much of the body's immune response is mounted in the lymph nodes. Cancer often spreads initially to these sites.

LYMPHATIC SYSTEM The lymph nodes and the structures that connect them, carrying lymph fluid from the periphery of the body back towards the heart.

MALIGNANCY Cancer.

METASTASIS The spread of cancerous cells from the site of origin to another part of the body. (plural—metastases)

OBTURATOR FOSSA An area near the prostate that contains the lymph nodes, which are usually the first site of spread.

ORCHIECTOMY The surgical removal of the testicles. (same as orchidectomy)

PALLIATION Treatment to improve quality of life and reduce suffering, particularly when cure is not a goal.

PARTIAL RESPONSE Disappearance of 50% or more of a detectable cancer.

PELVIC LYMPH NODE DISSECTION Removal of the lymph nodes draining the prostate to determine if they are cancerous.

PRIMARY CANCER The organ in which the cancer originated.

PROGRESSION Recurrence or growth of the disease, particularly in spite of treatment.

PROSTATE GLAND A spherical gland, just below the bladder, about the size of a walnut that secretes part of the seminal fluid and controls urinary flow.

PROSTATE-SPECIFIC ANTIGEN PSA An enzyme produced by the prostate that can be detected in blood.

PROSTATITIS Inflammation of the prostate.

PROSTHESIS An artificial device that is placed into the body or attached to the body as a substitute for a body part or lost function.

RADIATION THERAPY The use of x-rays for cancer treatment.

RADICAL PROSTATECTOMY The surgical removal of the entire prostate, including seminal vesicles and surrounding tissues.

RESECTION MARGIN The outside layer of the prostate evaluated following surgical removal. Positive margins means that cancer is seen at the outside edge of the prostate.

RESPONSE Reduction in the amount of cancer, usually in response to treatment.

RETROGRADE EJACULATION Backward flow of semen into the bladder during ejaculation. This may occur following a transurethral prostatectomy due to the loss of the closure of the bladder neck, which normally occurs.

RISK FACTOR A factor that is associated with an increased chance of being diagnosed with a disease. Examples include family history, diet, occupation, smoking.

SCREENING Testing that is done on a healthy person with no symptoms to see if they have an unsuspected disease.

SECONDARY CANCER See metastasis.

SEMEN (also known as seminal fluid) Spermatic fluid, which contains secretions from the testicles, prostate and seminal vesicles.

SPHINCTER A ring-like muscle, which acts as a valve.

STAGING Tests used to determine the extent of the cancer.

TRANSURETHRAL PROSTATECTOMY (TURP) An operation done through the urethra in which the prostate tissue obstructing the urethra is removed.

TUMOR An abnormal growth, which may be malignant or benign.

URETHRA The tube from the bladder to the penis through which urine or semen flows.

URETHRAL STRICTURE A narrowing of the urethra which may occur after surgery, inflammation or trauma.

VAS DEFERENS The tube carrying sperm from the testicles to the prostate gland.

**For fifty years, Coles Notes have been helping
students get through high school and university.
New Coles Notes will help get you through the rest of life.**

Look for these NEW COLES NOTES
and our NEW MEDICAL SERIES!

BUSINESS
- Effective Business Presentations
- Accounting for Small Business
- Write Effective Business Letters
- Write a Great Résumé
- Do A Great Job Interview
- Start Your Own Small Business
- Get Ahead at Work

GARDENING
- Indoor Gardening
- Perennial Gardening
- Herb Gardening
- Organic Gardening

LIFESTYLE
- Wine
- Bartending
- Wedding
- Opera
- Casino Gambling
- Better Bridge
- Better Chess
- Better Tennis
- Better Golf
- Public Speaking
- Speed Reading
- Cooking 101
- Scholarships and Bursaries
- Cats and Cat Care
- Dogs and Dog Care

PARENTING
- Your Child: The First Year
- Your Child: The Terrific Twos
- Your Child: Ages Three and Four
- Raising A Reader
- Helping Your Child in Math

PERSONAL FINANCE
- Basic Investing
- Investing in Stocks
- Investing in Mutual Funds
- Buying and Selling Your Home
- Plan Your Estate
- Develop a Personal Financial Plan

PHRASE BOOKS
- French
- Spanish
- Italian
- German
- Russian
- Japanese
- Greek

SPORTS FOR KIDS
- Basketball for Kids
- Baseball for Kids
- Soccer for Kids
- Hockey for Kids
- Gymnastics for Kids
- Martial Arts for Kids

**Coles Notes and New Coles Notes are available at the following stores:
Chapters • Coles • Smithbooks • World's Biggest Bookstore**